Kyudo

Kyudo

The Essence and Practice of Japanese Archery

HIDEHARU ONUMA

with Dan and Jackie DeProspero

KODANSHA INTERNATIONAL
Tokyo • New York • London

Distributed in the United States by Kodansha America, Inc.,
114 Fifth Avenue, New York, N.Y. 10011, and in the United Kingdom
and continental Europe by Kodansha Europe, Ltd., 95 Aldwych,
London WC2B 4JF.

Published by Kodansha International Ltd.,
17-14 Otowa 1-chome, Bunkyo-ku, Tokyo 112, and Kodansha America, Inc.

94 95 96 10 9 8 7 6 5 4 3 2
ISBN 4-7700-1734-0

Library of Congress Cataloging-in-Publication Data
Onuma, Hideharu, 1910-1990
    Kyudo : the essence and practice of Japanese archery / by Hideharu
 Onuma with Dan and Jackie DeProspero. — 1st ed.
    p.   cm.
    1. Archery—Japan,   2. Archery—Japan—Religious aspects.
3. Archery—Japan—Philosophy.   I. DeProspero, Dan.
II. DeProspero, Jackie.   III. Title.
GV1188.J3058 1992
799.3'2'0952—dc20
                            92-34073
                            CIP

For
Michael Hideharu
and
Mika Ann

Table of Contents

Acknowledgements

Shortly after we began our practice of kyudo, one of the senior instructors took us aside and offered this bit of advice: "Everything in kyudo is feeling," he said. At the time we did not entirely understand what he meant but it later proved to be a most important element of our study.

Learning anything new is difficult. Sometimes, learning kyudo can seem particularly so. The traditional Japanese method of instruction can be quite frustrating, especially to Westerners who all too often expect to be taught in a logical, orderly fashion. The Japanese tend toward loose interpretations of words. Often, that which remains unspoken is of more importance than what is voiced. On several occasions during the course of our study we have had to rely on intuition to discern the answer to a question we had posed. In time, as we became more comfortable with this method of instruction, we were able to rely more on our feelings. We asked fewer and fewer questions and put our trust in the teacher. If a correction were necessary, he would make it. If there was something we needed to know, we would be told.

To some this may seem like an unreasonable way to learn, but Onuma sensei liked to say that many things in kyudo are unreasonable. We must keep our body perfectly straight but have a round appearance, we must study technique but never use it, we should not pull the string when making the draw, and we must try not to release the arrow if we hope to hit the target. Unreasonable? Certainly, but it is up to us to find the "reasonableness" that lies hidden within the practice of kyudo. This book is an attempt to do just that. We hope that it will prove to be a reasonable source of information, instruction, and encouragement for all who are interested in kyudo.

We are indebted to a great number of people without whose help and encouragement this book would not have been possible. In particular we would like to thank Sato Kaori, *kyoshi*, 6th *dan* for providing the translations of the old family histories and for helping us to "read between the lines" of the text. And to Sugiyama Wataru and Tanaka Seiji, we say thank you for your patient efforts in translating endless pages of Japanese documents.

We are especially indebted to Fukuhara Ikuro, *hanshi*, 10th *dan*; Suhara Koun, Chief Priest at Engakuji-ha Zokutoan; Torii Shiro, professor at Gakushuin Daigaku Chutobu; and Takayanagi Noriaki, professor at Keio Gijuku Chutobu, for their support, encouragement, and professional guidance. We would also like to thank Ms. Sonia Katchian, who took the beautiful studio photographs of Onuma sensei that appear in Chapters 6 and 7.

We owe a special debt of gratitude to Osawa Kuwa, *hanshi*, 8th *dan*, and members of the Toshima-ku kyudojo for their help and kindness throughout our study of kyudo, and for their unending patience during the preparation of this book's contents. Also, a special mention must go to the Zen Nihon Kyudo Renmei for their continued support and assistance over the years.

To the Onuma family we say thank you for taking us in as one of your own, and for providing the mental and moral support that was necessary to see this book through to completion. Our very special thanks goes out to Ms. Takeko Minami, without whom we never would have made it to Japan in the first place; to Ed Nuhfer, long-time friend and confidant, whose constant encouragement helped make this book a reality; and to our parents who have endured our absence for so many years.

Finally, we are grateful to the staff of Kodansha International Ltd., publishers of this work, and we would especially like to thank our editor, Mr. Eric Chaline, for his guidance and enthusiastic support of this project.

It should be noted that all Japanese personal names are written in the traditional Japanese style of family name first. Also, for the sake of simplicity, diacritical marks and ideographs were intentionally omitted from the text. We would like to add that every effort was made to get as close to the heart of the teachings of Onuma sensei as was possible, and to see that this information was completely and accurately presented in this book. However, due to cross-cultural and linguistic differences, misunderstandings can sometimes occur. It is we alone, therefore, who must take responsibility for any factual errors or misinterpretations that may appear.

Dan and Jackie DeProspero

Preface

For several hundred years kyudo has served as the ideal expression of Japanese culture. Throughout history there has never been another culture that has so closely linked the act of shooting the bow with the condition of the human spirit. As important as this is to the Japanese, until recently very few Westerners have had the opportunity to study kyudo in depth. And fewer still have had access to the kind of knowledge one gets from a kyudo master. Mastery of kyudo begins with the study of technique but it does not end there. Only when one has attained a certain level of grace and dignity can one truly understand kyudo.

Onuma Hideharu was a man who possessed great dignity and grace. These qualities, coupled with his skill and knowledge of kyudo, made him the perfect model of a kyudo master. Add to this his knowledge of the English language and we find that no one was better qualified to explain kyudo to people living outside of Japan. Onuma sensei dedicated much of his life to spreading kyudo to the Western world. He traveled extensively to teach kyudo and welcomed many Westerners to his *kyudojo* here in Japan, one of whom was Dan DeProspero, who worked with Onuma sensei for many years on this book.

Mr. DeProspero is one of the very few Westerners who truly understand kyudo. He is one of those rare individuals who dedicate themselves wholeheartedly to the pursuit of excellence in their chosen field. His dedication clearly shows in the preparation of this book. Never before has so much information on kyudo been so clearly and accurately presented to the Western reader. His efforts have produced a book of unsurpassed quality that must be considered an indispensable source of information for anyone interested in gaining a greater understanding of kyudo and its dynamic expression of the spirit and culture of the Japanese people.

Fukuhara Ikuro, kyudo hanshi, *10th* dan
Zen Nihon Kyudo Renmei Deliberative Council Member,
Kanto Area Kyudo Renmei Rengo Kai President

Foreword

Onuma Hideharu devoted his entire life to the internationalization of kyudo. Because of this he was able to make hundreds of friends all over the world. I believe this book will be of great help to anyone interested in kyudo. And to all who admired Onuma sensei it will serve as a wonderful reminder of his teachings. Onuma sensei always taught *choshin*, the calming of the mind and spirit. Once you have read this book please be sure to do a few minutes of *choshin* before and after your practice. I trust then that *choshin* will create a beautiful rainbow that will connect kyudo practitioners all over the world.

When Onuma sensei was ill I visited him on a couple of occasions. Each time Dan DeProspero was there by his side, helping the Onuma family to care for him. When Onuma sensei passed away, I visited his home to read the sutras. Mr. DeProspero stayed in the room, listening to me read. I can still remember the serene look on his face. Later, Mr. DeProspero and the Onuma family asked me to write the foreword to this book. It was only then that I found out that Mr. DeProspero had been writing a book based on the teachings of Onuma sensei. Mr. De-Prospero lived with Onuma sensei for almost ten years. This enabled him to learn about kyudo not only through his practice sessions but also through his daily contact with Onuma sensei. Mr. DeProspero's life is centered around kyudo and the teachings of Onuma sensei. Now he has chosen to share these teachings with people throughout the world. I undertook the writing of this foreword because I trust in his ability to do just that.

This spring, when the white plum trees blossom, we will observe the anniversary of Onuma sensei's death. I am sure that the completion of this book will be the finest flower that one could take to his grave.

Suhara Koun, Chief Priest

Engakuji-ha Zokutoan
December 8, 1991
(The anniversary of Buddha's enlightenment)

Introduction

I was just a small boy when I began my study of Japanese archery. Perhaps it was due to my age, or maybe even the circumstances, but the method of instruction at that time was extremely simple: I was taught the fundamentals of shooting and then told to practice. My father did not give me detailed explanations, nor elaborate on the inner workings of the art. Instead, he expected me to watch him shoot and closely copy his manner. I now realize he was teaching me to rely less on intellect and more on the intuitive learning process.

Kyudo is full of paradoxes and hidden truths. Each day brings a new challenge which when met yields fresh insight. Even now, after more than seventy years of practice, I continue to be fascinated by the wonderful complexity of kyudo. Nevertheless, try not to think of kyudo as being difficult to learn. It is a fundamentally simple art consisting of just eight basic movements, and the shooting ceremony takes no more than a few minutes to complete. The practice of kyudo requires only that you align your body with the target, stand straight, fill yourself with spirit, and shoot with a pure heart and meaningful purpose.

This last point is of particular importance. In ancient times, when the bow was used for warfare or court ceremony, the archer concentrated on technique and etiquette. These are of course important elements of modern kyudo as well, but in this day and age we must aspire to a higher ideal.

In Japan we have a saying: "Act in accordance with the time and place." Life is no longer as simple as it once was. We live in a complex world where our very existence depends on continued peace and cooperation among all nations. The practice of kyudo cultivates balance and harmony. It is the means to better understand ourselves and one another.

My entire life has been devoted to the practice of Japanese archery. It has proved to be a worthwhile pursuit. Over the years I have had many wonderful experiences, made countless friends worldwide, and learned a great deal about myself in the process—no one can ask for more. This book is an attempt to share all I have learned in the hope that others will find it of value as well.

Hideharu Onuma

C H A P T E R
1

What is Kyudo?

Kyudo, the Way of the Bow, shares much in common with the Japanese tea ceremony (*chado*), calligraphy (*shodo*), swordsmanship (*iaido*), and the various other Ways which so effectively mirror the heart and mind of the Japanese. Kyudo is rich in history and tradition and is highly regarded in Japan. Many consider it to be one of the purest of all *budo* (martial ways). In the past, the bow was used for a variety of purposes: hunting, war, court games and rituals, religious ceremonies, and contests of skill. Many of these games and rituals survive to this day, but the Japanese bow long ago lost its practical value as a weapon. Today, kyudo is practiced primarily as a method of physical, moral, and spiritual development.

Kusajishi: ceremonial court game

Kyudo is often said to be like life itself: multifaceted and paradoxical. As such, it defies easy definition. Ask a novice practitioner what kyudo is and he or she will probably give you a detailed explanation of the technical or mental aspects of shooting. But ask a master of the art and he will usually reply with a simple, "I don't know." He is being neither evasive nor falsely modest. Instead, his answer reflects an understanding of the complexity and depth of kyudo. He realizes that even after a lifetime of study much of kyudo will remain enigmatic and unexplainable.

What, then, compels a man to spend fifty, sixty, or even seventy years practicing kyudo when he knows he can never really understand it? The answer, quite simply, is that he studies not so much to learn about the art as he does to learn about himself.

Truth, Goodness, and Beauty

Ever since he first acquired the ability to reason, man has sought to understand his humanity; to isolate and define those traits which separate him from other living things. Of course, he is blessed with a superior intellect, but what really sets man apart is his unlimited creative capacity. Many animals are builders and some can even fashion rudimentary tools, but man alone is capable of conceptual creation. The results of this ability—science, philosophy, religion, and art—are all the products of man's unique fascination with three elusive qualities: truth, goodness, and beauty. The pursuit of these qualities is a major element of the practice of kyudo.

The Search for Truth

Asking what is a true shot is one way of finding truth in kyudo. For most people this takes the form of the obvious; they equate true shooting with accuracy. Accuracy is, of course, important, and the ability to hit the target's center is basic to any form of archery, but kyudo makes a distinction between shooting that is merely skillful (*noshahichu*) and shooting that is correct and right-minded (*seishahichu*). The difference lies in how the center shot, known as *tekichu*, is obtained.

There are three progressively complex levels of *tekichu*: *toteki* (the arrow hits the target), *kanteki* (the arrow pierces the target), and *zaiteki* (the arrow exists in the target). In *toteki*, the archer concentrates on the technique of shooting. His goal is to reach a point where he can consistently hit the center mark. How he does this is generally of little consequence—the *toteki* archer is often unaware of, or chooses to ignore, the fact that his body lacks symmetry and his movements are dull and lifeless. Moreover, once he has found an accurate method of shooting, he is usually reluctant to change for fear that it will adversely affect his accuracy. Shooting that does not progress beyond this stage becomes little more than recreational diversion.

Emperor Jimmu depicted with the long bow

Nasu no Yoichi displays his skill at the battle of Yashima

Arrow makers during the medieval period (Tosa Mitsuoki)

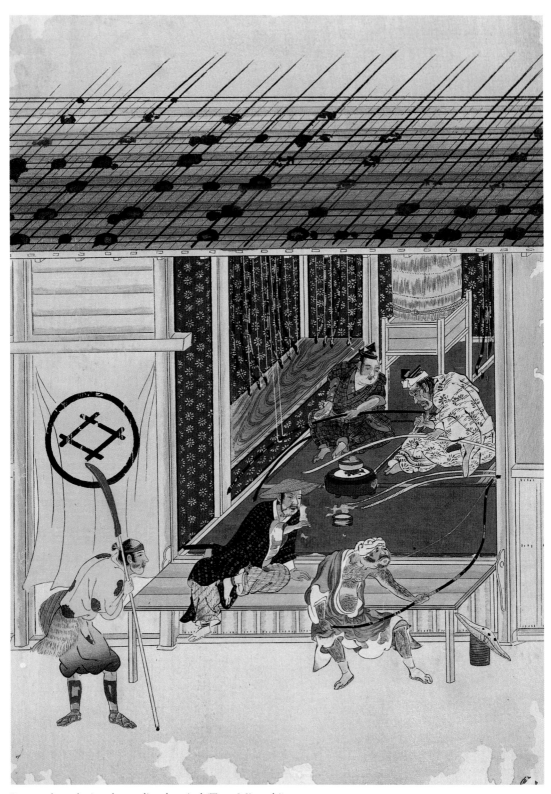

Bow makers during the medieval period (Tosa Mitsuoki)

The second level, *kanteki*, is considerably different. The *kanteki* arrow does not just hit the target, it pierces it. Originally, this was the method of the warrior archer who saw his target as a potential adversary. This type of shooting cannot be obtained through technical expertise alone; it requires an intensity that must come from somewhere deep within the archer himself. The *kanteki* archer is disciplined and well trained. He has, for the most part, mastered the physical skills of shooting and concentrates instead on the more obscure internal aspects, such as *kiai*— that peak moment when mind and body unify to create tremendous power—and breath control, which makes for smooth, yet vigorous, shooting.

Both *toteki* and *kanteki* are normal stages of development in kyudo, but the earnest practitioner does not stop at either one. In *zaiteki*, the highest level of *tekichu*, the target is neither goal nor opponent; instead, it is seen as an honest reflection of the self. Rather than focus on the target, the *zaiteki* archer concentrates on the quality of his thoughts and actions, knowing that if they can be made pure and calm, his body will naturally correct itself and the shooting will be true. To achieve this the archer must unify the three spheres of activity—mind (attitude), body (movement), and bow (technique)—which form the basis of shooting. When these three elements are unified, rational thinking gives way to feeling and intuition, the thoughts are quieted, and technique merges with the blood and the breath, becoming spontaneous and instinctive. The archer's body remains completely relaxed, yet is never slack. Always alert, his spirit pours forth, channeled into and beyond the ends of his bow and arrows until they become like natural extensions of his body. In this state it can be said that the arrow exists in the target prior to the release; there is no distance between man and target, man and man, and man and universe—all are in perfect harmony. This is true, right-minded shooting.

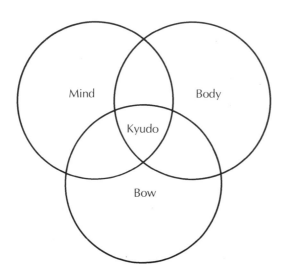

Truth is also expressed in the *tsurune*, the sound made by the bow-string. The sharp, high-pitched note produced by a smooth release is difficult to describe, but once heard it can never be forgotten. It is such a magical sound that the Japanese Imperial family traditionally heralds the birth of a child with repeated soundings of a bow in the belief that it will expel evil.

There is a story of a man who traveled throughout Japan in search of a kyudo teacher. One day as he walked through a small village he was surprised by the sound of a bow being shot from behind a garden wall. He knew immediately from the excellence of the *tsurune* that this was the master he had searched so long to find. He went to the garden and begged to be accepted as a student. His decision to study under this man was based entirely on the pureness of the string sound. This story illustrates how it is not always necessary to observe every aspect of shooting since in this one "moment of truth" the *tsurune* can reveal the quality of the shot.

Still another expression of truth in kyudo is *sae*. There is no single English word that can adequately describe this term; it can mean clear, bright, or even sharp. In the practice of kyudo it is used to describe shooting that is vivid and clear; shooting that is controlled but never rigid or strained.

Anyone who has ever tried to play a stringed instrument—a violin or cello, for example—knows that it takes precise control to produce a clear note. It is the same with kyudo. Correct posture, clean technique, and fluid movement all add up to shooting that has *sae*. *Sae* brings about a smooth, natural release of the string, and an arrow that flies straight and true and enters the target cleanly—much as a champion diver enters the water with a minimum of splash.

Because it lies deep within the human soul, the realization of truth has never been a simple matter. But *tekichu*, *tsurune*, and *sae* can provide us with a measure of our progress as we struggle to overcome our illusions of life and self. The bow never lies. It is honest and unbiased, an excellent teacher of truth.

The Importance of Goodness

Another important element of kyudo is goodness. The idea of goodness, which also includes such qualities as courtesy, compassion, morality, and nonaggression, is closely associated with the search for truth. When negative thoughts or actions enter into kyudo, the mind becomes clouded and the shooting is spoiled, making it impossible to separate fact from falsehood. Anger, for example, creates excessive tension in the body which makes for a forced release and dull *tsurune*. If the arrow happens to hit the target, chances are the archer will be left unaware of the poor quality of the shot simply because his mind and spirit were in a darkened state.

On the other hand, proper attitude and behavior, in combination with simple etiquette, create a state of mental and physical calmness that gradually becomes a normal part of daily life. This is called *heijoshin*, or ordinary mind. An ordinary mind is one that is calm, well balanced, and disciplined at all times—even when confronted with unexpected events or unpleasant circumstances. The secret to achieving *heijoshin* is to treat ordinary moments as special; then special events will seem like everyday occurrences. Once this happens we learn to avoid the pitfalls of hatred, vengeance, selfishness, and jealousy. We stop making excuses when our arrow fails to hit the target, and we show no resentment toward others whose shooting is better than our own. Instead, we look for what is missing in ourselves and, once discovered, spare no amount of time and energy to correct the deficiency.

It is often said that in this modern age the search for personal gratification has caused the human race to stray too far from traditional values. These days, it seems that courtesy and compassion have become marketable commodities; that people everywhere refuse to do anything for others unless they can expect some kind of compensation in return. If this is so, then perhaps kyudo, with its emphasis on introspection and self-improvement, can prompt each of us to examine our own motives for doing good and encourage us to extend a little kindness toward others simply because it is a good and proper thing to do.

The Beauty of Kyudo

Kyudo must also be beautiful. But since the concept of beauty varies between cultures it is difficult to define. All will agree, however, that it is a pleasant quality that enhances life and stimulates the spirit. The question is, how is beauty expressed in kyudo? Perhaps the first thing that strikes most people is the exquisite grace and artistry of the Japanese bow, coupled with the quiet elegance of the traditional attire worn by the archer. Indeed, it would be difficult to imagine a more aesthetically pleasing combination. But the real beauty of kyudo lies elsewhere.

First of all, truth and goodness are themselves beautiful. In their absence kyudo is ignoble and vulgar. There is nothing uglier than a person who becomes so concerned with hitting the target or showing off his skill that he loses sight of the truth. Even worse is someone who is corrupt and heartless, because these qualities destroy all that is beautiful in kyudo.

The kyudo ceremony, or more precisely the etiquette that lies at the heart of it, is also considered beautiful. Etiquette, which is basically just common courtesy and respect shown to others, gives the ceremony purpose. Without etiquette, the ceremony is stuffy and pretentious; the form, hollow and meaningless. In the kyudo ceremony, etiquette and serene, rhythmical movement combine to create a perfect balance of form and spirit. This, in turn, gives birth to harmony.

Harmony is particularly important because kyudo without the beauty of harmony is not really kyudo at all.

Grace, Dignity, and Tranquility

A formal kyudo ceremony is a study in elegance when performed by an experienced practitioner. Depending on the occasion and type of ceremony, the setting may or may not be elaborate, but in all cases the actions of the archer are simple and unassuming, and executed with utmost grace, dignity, and tranquility. These are the qualities that separate the true masters of the art from those merely skilled in shooting.

People have varied reasons for studying kyudo but above all they should use it to refine their character and mold themselves into better human beings. Of course, the practice of kyudo does not in itself guarantee us a more poised or dignified manner; that takes dedication and a strong desire for self-improvement. What it can do, though, is create numerous mental and physical challenges and encourage us—through the simple etiquette of the ceremony—to meet these challenges with grace and dignity, instead of overreacting in crude displays of negative behavior. If we practice sincerely it isn't long before we find ourselves acting in a more dignified and graceful manner in our daily lives as well.

Many people are drawn to kyudo by the calm, tranquil atmosphere that surrounds its practice. Tranquility comes when the archer learns to resolve the various mental and physical conflicts that arise during the practice of kyudo. Naturally, the more he is able to do this the better he is at creating a state of inner calmness, which is the root of tranquility. Smooth, rhythmical movement, controlled breathing, and concentration are very much a part of the process—as are dignity and grace.

Philosophical Influences

The combination of grace, dignity, and tranquility gives kyudo a solemn, religious-like quality, but kyudo is not a religion. It has, however, been influenced to a great extent by two major schools of Eastern philosophy: Shinto, the indigenous faith of Japan, and Zen, a sect of Buddhism imported from China.

Of the two philosophies the influence of Shinto, which is based on mythology and the belief in certain *kami*, or deities, is much older. Ritualistic use of the bow has been a part of Shinto for well over two thousand years. Further evidence of the long-standing relationship between kyudo and Shinto can be found in the ancient Shinto God of War, Hachiman, who is also known as the God of the Bow. It is also evident during the New Year's holidays when Shinto shrines offer symbolic white-feathered arrows as good-luck charms.

Kyudo ceremony at Meiji Jingu, Tokyo

Even more obvious is Shinto's influence on kyudo practice in general. Almost every visible aspect of modern kyudo—the ceremony, the manner of dress, and the respect shown for the bow, arrows, and shooting place—has been adapted from ancient Shinto thought and practice. This is especially apparent in the *kyudojo* (the shooting place) where the upper seat—the seat of honor—is also called the *kamiza*, or God's seat. Traditionally, the *kamiza* also housed the *kamidana*, a small Shinto altar. And though *kamidana* are no longer permitted in public *kyudojo* because of laws governing the separation of church and state, many private *kyudojo* still display the *kamidana* in recognition of the continuing bond between kyudo and Shinto.

It is Zen, though, that exerts the strongest philosophical influence on modern kyudo. Sayings like "One shot, one life" and "Shooting should be like flowing water" reveal the close relationship between the teachings of Zen and the practice of kyudo. Most of Zen's influence is relatively modern, however, dating back to about the seventeenth or eighteenth century, when Japan as a whole was at peace and the practice of kyudo took on a definite philosophical leaning. It was during this time that the concept of *bushido*, the Way of the Warrior, reached maturity. And it is generally thought that the word *kyudo* (the Way of the Bow) was first used in place of the word *kyujutsu* (the technique of the bow) during the same period. But the original relationship between kyudo and Zen did not begin here. During the Kamakura period (1185-1333), the samurai adopted Zen as their preferred method of moral training. Zen's lack of hard doctrine, coupled with its ascetic tendencies and emphasis on intuitive thinking, made it the perfect discipline for the Japanese warrior. It provided the samurai with the mental and moral support necessary to perform his

Kyudo at Engakuji Temple, Kamakura

duties, without passing judgment on him or his profession. Kyudo has changed dramatically since the days of the samurai, but the same aspects of Zen that once prepared the warrior archer for battle now enable modern practitioners of kyudo to better understand themselves and the world around them.

Endless Practice

Kyudo technique is not particularly difficult. The fundamentals of shooting are relatively easy to learn, and with a little practice, the ceremony, too, soon becomes second nature. But we do not practice kyudo merely to learn how to shoot a bow.

The saying "Whether one thousand arrows or ten thousand, each one must be new" captures the essence of kyudo. It means there can be no perfect shot, so we must never be satisfied when we have shot successfully. We must always strive to do better. In general, people fear change. They prefer to repeat their successes rather than risk failure. But in kyudo we are never disappointed by failure. Instead, we see it for what it really is: a learning experience that provides an opportunity for growth.

It is easy to understand the importance of not giving in to failure, but the idea of never allowing oneself to stop and savor success might seem foreign to some. It is this last concept, however, that separates kyudo from other forms of archery, where perfection is usually measured in terms of technical proficiency. A basic tenet of kyudo is that any shot, even one that is seemingly perfect, can be improved. Not on a technical level, because technical skill is limited—the body, no matter how well trained, will age, and physical ability will deteriorate accordingly. But the mind, or to be more precise, the spirit, has unlimited potential for improvement. The key to developing this potential is to understand that the practice of kyudo is endless; the reward comes not from the attainment of perfection, but from its unending pursuit.

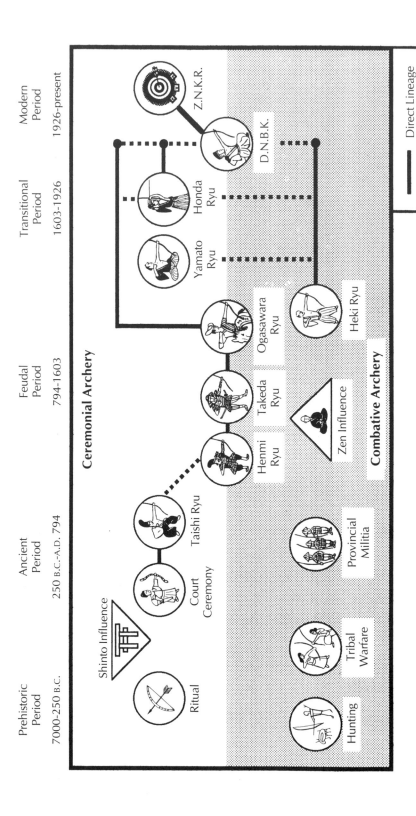

Historical development of modern kyudo

C H A P T E R

2

The History and Development of Kyudo

The history of Japanese archery continues to be the subject of scholarly discussion. The origins of kyudo are shrouded in myth and legend, and the records kept by the various clans are somewhat contradictory, reflecting a certain amount of familial bias. All this makes it extremely difficult to assemble a true historical picture. Nevertheless, enough similarities exist in the various ancient accounts to allow historians to piece together a fairly accurate historical record of kyudo.

The development of Japanese archery can be divided into five historical stages: the prehistoric period (from about 7,000 B.C. to A.D. 330), the ancient period (330-1192), the feudal period (1192-1603), the transitional period (1603-1912), and the modern period (1912 to the present).

The Prehistoric Period

Archaeological evidence shows that the earliest known inhabitants of the Japanese islands, a hunter-gatherer culture called the Jomon (7,000 B.C. to 250 B.C.), relied heavily on the use of the bow. While it is probable that they used the bow for tribal warfare, and possibly for ritual as well, it was primarily used for hunting. The bow was, in fact, the most sophisticated tool that early Japanese man possessed.

The period which followed, from about 250 B.C. to A.D. 330, was dominated by the Yayoi culture. This was the beginning of the iron age in Japan, and life in the village changed dramatically. The Yayoi spent more time working in the village than did the Jomon, and this helped to strengthen the sense of community among the villagers. Also, historians believe that the more powerful families began to exact tribute from the villagers, thus initiating a system of political and economic control over the whole community. The villagers were now forced to spend even more time fishing and farming and less time hunting in order to meet the demands put upon them. As a result, the first of a series of transformations in the way the bow was used occurred: It evolved from a hunting tool into a symbol and instrument of political power.

The exact date of the establishment of the first centralized system of government is unknown. Legend says that Emperor Jimmu ascended to the throne in 660 B.C., but most historians now dismiss this date as myth. Citing Chinese and Korean sources, they believe that the first Japanese state was established no earlier than the third or fourth century. What's more, recent thinking casts doubt on the belief that Jimmu was Japan's first emperor.

The question of Jimmu's existence is a subject outside the scope of this book, but it is interesting to note that in paintings and descriptions of his life, Jimmu is always depicted with a long bow and arrows. This clearly illustrates that even in the earliest stages of the development of the Japanese state the bow was used as a symbol of authority and political unity.

The Ancient Period

From the fourth to the ninth century, Chinese culture strongly influenced the system of government in Japan. Along with etiquette and court ritual, the Japanese adopted the ceremonial archery of the Chinese aristocracy, which considered proficiency in archery the mark of a refined, well-educated man. A scholar of the time wrote that civilized men should never fight to settle their differences but should resolve them through a test of shooting skill. Such contests must be governed by a strict code of etiquette, and both participants must conduct themselves accordingly. They must show their respect by bowing to one another before they shoot, and afterward, the loser must accept the results with dignity and grace, and offer a toast of congratulations to the winner.

Chinese court archer

Japan and China broke off relations in the ninth century, but Chinese thought continued to have a profound and lasting influence on Japanese archery. In fact, long after ceremonial archery died out in China it continued to develop in Japan, where it ultimately flowered into the art of kyudo.

The following three hundred years brought several changes that once again altered the practice of Japanese archery. First of all, as the power of privileged landowners increased, they were granted tax exemptions and immunity from official inspectors. An increasing amount of land thus passed into true private holdings. Then, as the state's authority over the land diminished, landowners assumed the responsibility of governing and protecting the people who lived within their private estates. As a result, the conscript army, an undisciplined and poorly trained group of men who were more laborer than soldier, was replaced by a more capable provincial militia. Finally, as the influence of the central government waned, the power of the elite warrior families increased and a new military class, the samurai, began to dominate the country. The rise of the samurai class led to the formation of the various *ryu*, or martial schools. The early archery *ryu* were not very organized; they had no systematic methods of instruction. Nevertheless, they provided training for new generations of archers. Consequently, the major samurai clans came to depend heavily on the expertise of the archery schools.

There is historical mention of a "Taishi Ryu" that supposedly existed during the regency of Shotoku Taishi (593-622), but it is generally thought that the Henmi Ryu, which was founded about five hundred years later by Henmi Kiyomitsu, was the first archery *ryu*. It was followed by the Takeda Ryu and the Ogasawara Ryu, both of which were established by descendants of Kiyomitsu.

Ogasawara Ryu

The struggle for supremacy among the samurai clans led to a confrontation between the two main families, the Minamoto and Taira (the Gempei War, 1180-1185), and as a result the use of the bow increased dramatically.

There are numerous stories from that time that tell of the exploits of warrior archers. Two of the most famous tales concern Minamoto no Tametomo and Nasu no Yoichi.

Minamoto no Tametomo was said to have been an exceptionally large and powerful man. It is recorded that his arrows measured "twelve hands and two fingers." He supposedly used a bow that was so powerful it took five men to pull it. Legend has it that during the Gempei era, Tametomo lived in exile on Oshima island in Izu. Since he considered the island to be his private domain, he refused to pay taxes. His intransigence ultimately provoked the central government into sending an armada of twenty small warships in an attempt to force him to pay. As a gesture of defiance, Tametomo decided to shoot a large, bulbed arrow over the bow of one of the ships, but it struck the wooden hull a few inches above the waterline instead. The shot was so powerful that the arrow penetrated both sides of the vessel, creating two gaping holes. Sea water poured in and the ship began to sink. The sight of a warship being sunk by a single arrow so frightened the other ships' captains that they made an immediate retreat.

Nasu no Yoichi is a popular figure in the arts and literature of Japan, but as with Minamoto no Tametomo, accounts of his life are probably somewhat exaggerated. Nasu no Yoichi is best known for his exceptional display of skill at Yashima, a decisive battle between the Minamoto and Taira. A powerful Minamoto army forced the Taira to retreat to their ships just off the Inland Sea coast, and in the ensuing battle most of the fleet was lost. However, the Taira would not accept defeat without issuing one last symbolic challenge. They

Minamoto no Tametomo

anchored one of their remaining ships about seventy meters offshore and challenged the Minamoto archers to hit a small folding fan tied to the top of a long wooden staff. Nasu no Yoichi, the greatest Minamoto archer, took up the challenge. On horseback, and in full view of both friend and foe, he rode a short distance into the choppy sea and prepared to shoot. He asked the gods to calm the wind and guide his shot. Miraculously, the wind died down and the sea stilled. Nasu no Yoichi raised his bow, took careful aim, and let the arrow fly. It arced toward the Taira ship and sliced through the base of the fan, toppling it into the sea. After a moment's silence the warriors from both sides roared with approval.

The Gempei War produced many exceptional fighting men like Minamoto no Tametomo and Nasu no Yoichi, and firmly established the *bushi*, or samurai, as a powerful new social class. The ascent of the samurai was to prove significant in the development of Japanese archery.

The Feudal Period

In 1192 Minamoto no Yoritomo, the head of the Minamoto clan, was granted the title of shogun. By this time he had successfully consolidated his power and more or less controlled the entire country from his headquarters in Kamakura. The Kyoto Imperial Court remained in place, but was eventually forced to relinquish all authority to the military regime. It was only natural, then, that the principles and practices of the military should influence the whole of society.

Yabusame: Ogasawara Ryu

Near the end of the twelfth century, Yoritomo initiated stricter training standards for his warriors. As part of the training he instructed Ogasawara Nagakiyo, the founder of Ogasawara Ryu, to teach mounted archery. Shooting from horseback was certainly not new but this was the first time it was taught in a more or less standardized way. In the years that followed, *yabusame*, or mounted archery, would reach its full potential, thus adding a new dimension to the study of kyudo.

For most of the fifteenth and sixteenth centuries Japan was troubled by civil war. It was a destructive period, but it let the samurai hone their fighting skills on an almost constant basis, producing some of the finest warriors in Japanese history. Subsequently, the bow gained even more importance as a weapon and the technique of shooting improved significantly.

One of the most influential archers of the time was Heki Danjo Masatsugu, a warrior of exceptional skill and reputation. There is little written about Heki Danjo, and historians disagree on the facts surrounding his life. Most think that he lived in both Yamato (modern-day Nara prefecture) and Iga (modern-day Mie prefecture), but some maintain that there were actually two different Heki families, one in Yamato and the other in Iga. In spite of all the confusion, most historians agree that Heki Danjo actually existed. It is generally thought that he was born in 1443 and died at the age of fifty-nine. According to legend, Heki Danjo was almost forty years old when he had a revelation about the working of the bow which he called "*Hi, Kan, Chu*" (Fly, Pierce, Center). After experimenting with various ways of holding and drawing the bow, Heki Danjo discovered a new and devastatingly accurate method of shooting that completely revolutionized the course of Japanese archery.

Prior to Heki Danjo, shooting styles varied greatly and there was little in the way of formalized teaching, especially in the case of battlefield technique. Archers mostly trained on their own, adopting whatever methods they felt were most effective. The samurai were quick to recognize the potential of Heki Danjo's shooting style, however, so it did not take long for his method to spread.

Heki Danjo passed his secrets on to Yoshida Shigekata. Shigekata's descendants formed their own factions and, in time, the number of schools based on the teachings of Heki Danjo increased to about twelve in all. This included the Chikurin-ha (Chikurin school) which evolved from Iga Heki Ryu, most likely through a member of the Yoshida family. These schools were called "new schools," in contrast to the Henmi, Takeda, and Ogasawara Ryu which had dominated both court and battlefield archery until the appearance of Heki Danjo.

It is generally thought that a great number of archery schools existed in ancient times, but most were actually branches of Heki Ryu—with the exception of the old schools, of course—and many, such as

Heki Danjo Masatsugu

Hideharu Onuma, 15th-generation headmaster of Heki Ryu Sekka-ha

Heki Ryu Chikurin-ha, Heki Ryu Sekka-ha, and Heki Ryu Insai-ha, continue to this day.

The use of the bow reached a peak during the fifteenth and sixteenth centuries. Teaching methods were refined and codified, and bow and arrow manufacturing techniques were perfected. During this period the archer held a high position in the warrior hierarchy. But all this was to change suddenly on August 25, 1543, when a Chinese frigate ran aground at Tanegashima in southern Kyushu. On board were three Portuguese armed with muskets—a weapon previously unknown to the Japanese. While the proud samurai were at first disgusted at the thought of using these foreign weapons, it wasn't long before the Japanese began manufacturing guns in large quantities. In 1575, the warlord Oda Nobunaga was the first to successfully use firearms in a major battle, thus ending the bow's usefulness as a weapon of war.

The Transitional Period

Early in the seventeenth century, Shogun Tokugawa Ieyasu managed to unify the warring samurai factions, and the nation settled into a long period of peace. The absence of war, coupled with the introduction of firearms, should have caused the samurai archers to abandon the bow completely, but they refused to do so. Sensing that *kyujutsu*—the technique of fighting with a bow—was on the verge of becoming obsolete, they set up a regular competition at Sanjusangendo Temple in Kyoto in hopes of reviving interest in archery.

At Sanjusangendo, the archers, from a seated position, were required to shoot down a long, narrow corridor at a target placed some 120 meters away. Low-hanging wooden beams made the shot even more difficult, as evidenced by the scores of arrow shafts that remain imbedded in the beams to this day. Up to the end of the Edo period, 823 archers took up the Sanjusangendo challenge, but fewer than

Sanjusangendo Temple, Kyoto

Arrows imbedded in the beams at Sanjusangendo

thirty left any record of note. Among these, two archers stand alone: Hoshino Kanzaemon and Wasa Daihachiro.

Hoshino Kanzaemon was so worried about the state of archery that he took it upon himself to travel the country and study archery technique. He was determined to be the best archer of his time. His dedication payed off. By the middle of the seventeenth century, when he took part in the competition at Sanjusangendo, no one could rival his shooting. Hoshino's record of 8,000 hits—out of a total of 10,542 arrows shot—stands as a testimony to his skill.

As amazing as Hoshino Kanzaemon's record was, it would be bettered seventeen years later by Wasa Daihachiro, an archer of great strength and stamina. A story has it that when Wasa Daihachiro made his attempt, he took a break after several hours of constant shooting. When he returned he was no longer able to shoot as before; his arrows would not even travel the length of the corridor. At that point, an older samurai who had been standing nearby watching him shoot approached and chided him for stopping. The man took a small knife and made a number of tiny cuts on Wasa Daihachiro's left hand, which had become so gorged with blood that he could no longer hold the bow properly. Once the pressure was released, Wasa Daihachiro regained his strength and went on to surpass all previous attempts. He did not find out till later that the man who had helped him break Hoshino's record was Hoshino Kanzaemon himself.

In a twenty-four hour period—shooting from one evening into the next—Wasa Daihachiro shot 13,053 arrows and made 8,133 hits. This averages out to about nine arrows per minute, or one every six or seven seconds—an unbelievable record that almost surely will never be equalled.

Despite all their efforts, however, the samurai clans failed to restore *kyujutsu* to its former glory. Times had changed, and the bow would never again be used in battle.

In the latter half of the seventeenth century, the general populace took up the practice of archery in increasing numbers, and ceremonial shooting became prevalent. According to some sources, Morikawa Kozan, the founder of modern Yamato Ryu, first coined the word "kyudo" about this time. And although it would take nearly two hundred years for the term to gain widespread acceptance, continued peace and the introduction of newer, more efficient firearms made it inevitable that the emphasis of archery training would shift toward mental and spiritual development.

The Meiji era (1868-1912) saw Japan embark on a course of rapid modernization. Suddenly, everything European was in fashion. Naturally, traditional culture suffered, and Japanese archery was in danger of disappearing.

Near the turn of the century Honda Toshizane, a kyudo instructor at Tokyo Imperial University, combined elements of the warrior and ceremonial styles to create a hybrid method of shooting, which he taught to his students. Until this time the teachings of the two styles were more or less separate. Of course, the traditional schools did not support the new method. Their protests went largely unheard, however, as Honda Toshizane continued to teach his students the hybrid style. As time went by, his teachings spread outside the school system, and Honda Ryu—as it later came to be known—found favor with the general public. Today, Honda Toshizane is recognized as being one of the most influential kyudo masters of modern times. Some say that he was not only responsible for changing the direction of Japanese archery but also for ensuring its survival into the twentieth century.

The Modern Period

Now that kyudo was no longer under the total control of the traditional archery families, and more and more people were coming together to practice kyudo, it became necessary to establish some sort of national shooting standard. In the early 1930s the Dai Nippon Butoku Kai (Great Japan Martial Virtues Association) invited the various schools to participate in the formation of such a standard. The issue was highly controversial and was debated for quite some time before a tentative agreement was finally reached in 1934. And although the new standards were largely ignored by the major schools of archery, kyudo experienced a revival in popularity that would last until the end of World War II.

After the war, the practice of kyudo and other martial arts was banned by the occupation forces. But in 1946 various kyudo masters and other influential persons successfully lobbied GHQ for permission to form a new kyudo organization. The first attempt to reorganize did not meet with the approval of the occupation authorities, however, and it was not until 1949 that final authorization was granted to form the Zen Nihon Kyudo Renmei (All Japan Kyudo Federation). In the summer of 1953 the Zen Nihon Kyudo Renmei published the Kyudo Kyohon (manual), which set forth the modern standards of form, etiquette, and shooting procedure. Since that time the *sharei*, or shooting ceremony, has been steadily refined, and the number of people practicing kyudo has risen to over 500,000 worldwide.

In the fall of 1989, men and women from eight different countries, ranging in age from the mid-teens to ninety-nine, gathered at the Budokan in Tokyo to celebrate the fortieth anniversary of the Zen Nihon Kyudo Renmei. Their presence, and the fact that they could shoot together in harmony, stands as living testimony to the strengths of modern kyudo. It also shows that Japanese archery has truly evolved from a method of defeating one's enemies into a way of promoting lasting friendship and world peace.

CHAPTER
3

The Spirit of Kyudo

A popular saying in kyudo goes: "Shooting with technique improves the shooting, but shooting with spirit improves the man." In a similar vein, Anzawa Heijiro, a respected kyudo master, liked to say that shooting is a means to improve our personality, and those who dwell excessively on technique lose sight of the Way.

Kyudo cannot be learned through technique alone; we must never forget the importance of the inner self when practicing. An old proverb tells us: " A wise man is never puzzled, a benevolent man is never troubled, and a courageous man is never afraid." It means we must believe in ourselves because deep within us all there exists a power that allows us to overcome inherent human weaknesses and reach our full potential. The Japanese call this power *shinki;* in the West we call it spirit.

The Working of the Spirit

Because the practice of kyudo involves very little physical activity, spirit is extremely important. If the spirit is weak, the shooting becomes dull and shallow, without any vitality whatsoever. In kyudo one should be like a deep-flowing river, calm and steady on the surface but with tremendous power hidden in the depths, and not like a small stream, which, because of its noise and turbulence, seems powerful but is really weak in comparison. To further illustrate this point, kyudo masters often cite the following proverb: "A mighty dragon cannot live in shallow water." The analogy is simple: Experience and depth of character are the source of a strong spirit.

If we examine the term "*shinki*" we find that it is made up of two concepts: *shin* (heart or mind) and *ki* (vital energy). According to Japanese thought, *ki* is ever present and readily available to all, but it takes a strong, stable mind to fully harness its power. Thus, strict self-control and emotional stability are essential to the practice of kyudo.

There are some who argue that any attempt to control the human spirit stifles creativity. They find themselves unable to adhere to the strict guidelines and ceremonial procedures so typical of the traditional Japanese arts, and prefer a more casual approach. Such an attitude is usually a cover for insufficient skill, however, so real technique is replaced with ostentatious display and unorthodox methods—all in the name of creativity. But true creativity is sister to the spirit, and both are born of simplicity. Neither can be learned, like some school subject, nor can they be feigned. They are not a product of the intellect, but flower only when the analytical mind is quieted and the intuitive thought process takes over.

Most people believe that the teaching is kept simple and the ceremony strictly controlled to ensure that the techniques are transmitted correctly from generation to generation. That is partly true, but a deeper reason exists: Limiting the student to a certain pattern of movement forces him or her to discard all extraneous action and thought and move into a state of consciousness known as *mushin* (no mind).

For most of us, the concept of *mushin* seems foreign because we associate "no mind" with no thought—the equivalent of unconsciousness or even death. But *mushin* is not the elimination of thought, it is the elimination of the remnants of thought: that which remains when thought is divorced from action. In *mushin*, thought and action occur simultaneously. Nothing comes between the thought and the action, and nothing is left over.

When explained in simple, straightforward terms, *mushin* does not seem particularly difficult to understand. Still, people who have actually experienced *mushin*—through the practice of Zen or the martial arts—caution against intellectual acceptance of *mushin* without firsthand experience. They compare it to a man describing what it's like to give birth. He may be able to sympathize with the pain and appreciate the wonder of it all, but because he lacks the experience of giving birth, he can never truly understand it in the same sense that a woman does.

That is why a master kyudo instructor keeps his explanations to a minimum and encourages his students to find the answers for themselves. He knows that overteaching only further stimulates the intellect and inhibits intuition, thus denying the student the chance to experience the hidden, inner workings of the art.

The Importance of Balanced Effort

To qualify for ranking and teaching licenses in modern kyudo, an individual must pass a series of practical, written, and oral examinations. At the higher levels, one of the more difficult questions asks for an explanation of the connection between breath and *kiai*, the moment when the spirit is working at its fullest. Most of the respondents divide their answer into two parts: a description of proper breathing technique, followed by examples of how it contributes to the development of the spirit. Such answers reveal little about the true relationship between the breath and spirit, however.

Every so often, though, someone answers in a way that reflects a deep, intuitive understanding of the question. That respondent realizes that, in truth, breath and spirit are one and the same. And that we tend to think of them as separate because the act of breathing is a part of physical reality and easily observed, while the working of the spirit is far less tangible. Since they are one, however, we can use our knowledge of the breath to better understand the spirit.

We know that in a healthy person breathing is smooth, rhythmical, and constant. Day in and day out the lungs take in life-sustaining oxygen and send it through the bloodstream to every part of the body. At the same time, harmful gases are carried back to the lungs to be expelled. The whole process is such an integral part of us that we tend to forget how vitally important it is. Only when the breath weakens or stops altogether do we give it any notice.

It is the same with the spirit. As long as it flows smoothly, a person will remain strong and full of life. But the moment it is diminished or fails, that person becomes vulnerable, both physically and mentally. The Japanese call this condition *suki*.

Being human, we will probably always be vulnerable to some degree. Nevertheless, a major aspect of kyudo training is learning how to discipline our mind and body and eliminate *suki*. But because it is impossible to separate the working of the spirit from that of the body, most people have a tendency to substitute physical strength for mental effort. They believe they can overcome their weaknesses by physical training alone. Physical training can make the body strong but it does not eliminate *suki*.

Suki means opening or gap. Physically, it occurs when strength is applied excessively at particular points in the body while the remaining areas are ignored. And since no one can keep every muscle in his or her body tensed indefinitely, people who rely solely on physical strength are always prone to excessive *suki*. This does not mean that physical strength is unnecessary, only that we must learn to use our strength naturally. Natural means balanced. Too much or too little of anything—even food, water, or sunshine—is unnatural. In kyudo, we must learn to balance our use of strength by evenly distributing it throughout the body, and use only the strength necessary to accomplish the task at hand—no more, no less.

More than anything else, though, *suki* is a condition of the mind. All weakness, even physical weakness, can be directly linked to unbalanced mental effort. We all know that when we are involved in any serious undertaking, total concentration is absolutely necessary. What we fail to realize, however, is that our efforts to concentrate completely often become excessive and we tip the balance in the opposite direction. We become so engrossed in the process that we move from a state of awareness, in which we are extremely alert yet calm and undisturbed by sudden movement or unexpected events, into a trance-like state where we lose all sensitivity to the world around us.

The idea of *suki* and balanced mental and physical effort is difficult to explain, but there is a simple story that has been used for generations to help teach the concepts:

In ancient times, the sport of cock fighting was as popular with the Japanese nobility as horseracing was with their European counterparts. And, like horseracing, a great deal of time and expense was invested in the acquisition and training of a champion cockerel.

It happened that the emperor himself greatly enjoyed the sport. Naturally, it was important for him to have the best fighting bird in all the land. He sent his finest rooster to a master trainer and instructed him not to return the bird until it was unbeatable. The trainer accepted the task but cautioned that it might take a good deal of time to complete the training.

When, after several weeks, no word had come from the trainer, the emperor summoned him to the court. "Is my bird ready to fight?" asked the emperor.

"Not yet, sire," replied the trainer. "When I set him opposite another bird he gets frightened and jumps about nervously. Please give me a little more time."

A few more weeks passed and the trainer was once again called to the palace to report to the emperor.

"Sire, your bird is still not quite ready," he said. "He has become a strong, skillful fighter, but he is too aggressive. His eyes are filled with hate, and his heart is filled with desire."

The emperor was losing his patience. He ordered the trainer to intensify his efforts.

Some time later, the emperor decided to pay the trainer a surprise visit. The trainer's reputation was impeccable, but he was taking much too long to train the bird, and the emperor was beginning to doubt his ability. The emperor demanded to see the bird fight, so it was brought to the center of the garden and placed opposite an equally skilled fighting cock. They stood ready to fight. The emperor's bird puffed its feathers, thrust out its chest, and strutted confidently toward its opponent. Suddenly, the other bird attacked and a vicious fight ensued. The fight continued for several minutes before the emperor's bird emerged victorious.

The emperor was delighted. "You've done an excellent job," he told the trainer. "I'll take him back with me now."

The trainer protested: "Please, sire, not yet. He is not ready to fight for you."

"Nonsense," replied the emperor, "he fought extremely well."

"I know," said the trainer, "but he is too arrogant. And his arrogance is his weakness."

The trainer's sincerity convinced the emperor to let him finish training the bird.

Finally, the trainer showed up at the palace with the cock and announced to the emperor that the training was complete.

"Quick, set him down," said the emperor. " I want to see him fight."

The bird was placed on the ground before the emperor. It stood strong and alert, but remained motionless—not a feather moved, nor an eye blinked.

"What have you done to him?" the emperor demanded. "He looks like he is made of wood."

The trainer motioned for his assistants to bring in several fighting cocks. Each, in turn, was placed on the ground to fight. The emperor watched in amazement as, one by one, the birds ran away, frightened by the mere presence of this majestic "wooden" bird.

Needless to say, the emperor was extremely pleased, and he rewarded the trainer handsomely.

Discovering the True Self

We all have a natural need for balance in our lives. Consequently, we spend a great deal of our time searching for it along various paths: religion or philosophy, the arts, our work, recreation, or family and friendships. Though they may seem diverse, these paths all share a common ground: They add value and purpose to our lives and provide us with love, security, hope, and a sense of self-worth. In short, they help us deal with the challenges of life.

Kyudo is also one of life's paths, and it too can help us find balance, but kyudo by itself does not solve our problems nor add anything to our lives—at least not in the beginning. Instead, the practice of kyudo methodically peels away the protective layers of ego that we hide behind, until our true nature is revealed. Simply put, kyudo exposes our shortcomings. It is then up to us to make a thorough self-examination and balance our character accordingly. Thus, kyudo works in perfect harmony with the other paths. It is not meant to replace any of them, but it very nicely complements them all.

However, because the bow was once a weapon of war, and kyudo itself is considered a martial art, some people question how the spirit of kyudo can be compatible with the spirit of friendship or religion. They contend that the martial spirit has more in common with the spirit of competitive sport. Their skepticism is understandable. After all, many modern sports are based on the skills of ancient warriors. What's more, since contests have always been a part of Japanese archery, it seems only natural for kyudo practitioners to have a strong competitive spirit.

Certainly, everyone who practices kyudo would rather hit the target than miss it; but since the target is only paper and wood, and the Japanese bow is no longer used for hunting or war, shooting simply for the sake of hitting the target seems rather meaningless. Kyudo addresses the problem by encouraging us to view the target as a reflection of our strengths and weaknesses, and to use the shooting to discover our true selves. That perspective puts our competitive instincts to positive use, and gives the act of shooting deeper meaning. Sometimes we will hit the target but miss the self. At other times we will miss the target but hit the self. Our purpose, though, is to hit the target as the self, and hope that the sharp sound of arrow penetrating paper will awaken us from the so-called "dream of life" and give us real insight into the ultimate state of being.

C H A P T E R
4

The Shooting Place

A *kyudojo* (shooting place) can be simple or grand, anything from a single target suspended before a mound of dirt to an elaborate complex on the grounds of a shrine or temple. But size and architectural differences aside, all true *kyudojo* share one thing in common: They are not just places to shoot arrows, they are places to contemplate the true condition of the self. Consequently, the moment we walk into a *kyudojo* we must be prepared to leave behind our worldly cares and enter into serious study.

Koryusai (c. 1770)

Shiseikan Kyudojo at Meiji Jingu, Tokyo

Enma Kyudojo at Engakuji, Kamakura

Respect, Harmony, and Etiquette

A *kyudojo* is a place of focus for individuals with common values and a common purpose. Therefore, anyone entering the *kyudojo* is expected to adhere to a common standard of behavior based on respect, harmony, and simple etiquette.

Most cultures have a tradition of showing respect for certain types of structures: the home, places of worship, or schools, for example. It is not unusual, then, for the Japanese to exhibit a high degree of respect for the *kyudojo*. Naturally, traditional customs, like bowing when entering or leaving the *kyudojo* and removing one's shoes before going inside, are followed. But there are other ways to show respect for the *kyudojo*. One is to keep it immaculately clean; it is the responsibility of every student to assist with the daily sweeping and dusting of the *kyudojo*. Another way is to constantly practice self-restraint while in the *kyudojo* so as not to disturb the tranquility of the place. That does not mean, however, that we cannot talk or move about in the *kyudojo;* quiet conversation and activity is permissible. But loud, raucous behavior is completely unacceptable. It is not only disruptive but highly disrespectful as well.

Contrary to popular belief in the West, the atmosphere in a *kyudojo* is not particularly severe or restrictive. Actually, the *kyudojo* is charged with positive energy. It is always warm and welcoming, a place of absolute harmony. Here, the individual is considered to be less important than the group. Therefore, patience, cooperation, humility, and a willingness to temper one's personal desires are qualities that every student of kyudo must cultivate for the good of the entire *kyudojo* community.

Many *kyudojo* start the day's practice with a few minutes of meditation. The reason is twofold: First, it allows all the members of the *kyudojo* to purge their minds of mundane thoughts and calm themselves before practice. Second, it is the perfect way to bring together in harmony individuals of varied professions and personalities. It is from this quiet beginning that we learn to blend harmoniously with our surroundings even as we progress from the relative simplicity of daily practice to the complexities of life outside the *kyudojo*.

Anyone familiar with Japanese culture will understand the importance of etiquette in the *kyudojo*. Etiquette, after all, governs nearly every aspect of life in Japan. However, first-time visitors need not feel apprehensive about entering the *kyudojo* because apart from a few distinctly Japanese social conventions *kyudojo* etiquette is the same as etiquette everywhere. Therefore, simple politeness coupled with common sense will suffice. Later, if the individual decides to become a permanent member of the group, he or she will be instructed in the particulars of *kyudojo* behavior: How and when to bow, where to sit or stand, and when to help with some of the small tasks that are a part of life in the *kyudojo*.

Meditation before practice, Toshima-ku Kyudojo, Tokyo

Etiquette, respect, and harmony are inseparably linked. Together they create a most wonderful atmosphere in the *kyudojo:* a feeling of warmth and serenity and fellowship that radiates from the very heart of the *kyudojo* and touches all who visit it.

The Different Types of *Kyudojo*

If given the choice, most of us would prefer to practice kyudo in an elegant wooden structure set in a spacious garden. But in today's world this is not always possible. All too often, space and financial limitations force us into a compromise between our dreams and the realities of modern life. The problem is not new, however. Archers of the past faced many of the same limitations. They too found it necessary to practice kyudo in a variety of locations, both indoors and outdoors, in spaces large and small—almost any place with room enough for the bow to be drawn and the arrow released.

The *Makiwara Kyudojo*

When space is at a premium, kyudo is practiced at a *makiwara*, a tightly bound drum of straw. Because we shoot at the *makiwara* at close range—only a bow's length away—it can be set up in a relatively small space: a section of the garden, a corner of a porch, or even a spare room with a high ceiling. Sometimes, though, several *makiwara* are housed in a structure of their own where formal classes, complete with all the ceremony and etiquette of normal kyudo practice, are taught. This is a *makiwara kyudojo*, and aside from the fact that the arrows are only shot a short distance it is the same as any other *kyudojo* and should be treated as such.

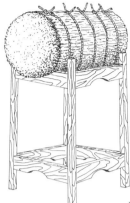

Makiwara: straw practice target

Makiwara practice

The Single-Target *Kyudojo*

The single-target *kyudojo* is probably the best choice for individuals who have adequate space but limited finances. The layout of this type of *kyudojo* is quite basic: a platform from which to shoot, a clear pathway for the arrow's flight, and a simple backdrop of straw or earth.

More often than not, a single-target *kyudojo* is built in the open. However, if finances permit, a simple enclosure can be erected over the shooting and target areas to protect them from the elements. In the latter case, a full-length mirror, equipment stands, and various other accessories can be added. Also, if there is sufficient space, a *makiwara* can be set up at the back of the shooting platform.

Single-target *kyudojo*, Tucson, Arizona

The Standard *Kyudojo*

A standard *kyudojo* is designed so that archers in groups of three, four, five, or multiples of five can shoot together at individual targets. Shooting of this type is more demanding than private practice because each archer must coordinate his or her own actions with those of other group members.

A standard *kyudojo* consists of a *shajo* (shooting hall), a *yamichi* (arrow pathway), and a *matoba* (target house). The layout is similar to a single-target *kyudojo* but the design of the structures is much more complex.

The *shajo* is a large, open-faced building with a polished wooden floor and a ceiling at least 3.8 meters high. The floor should be five meters or more in width and long enough to allow at least 1.8 meters between the archers. The standard distance between the shooting position and the target is twenty-eight meters. The *shajo* itself can be constructed of any material, but the floor is traditionally made of Japanese cypress or cedar. These two woods provide an excellent surface for the practice of kyudo; they combine a firm, sure footing with beauty, warmth, and durability.

All *shajo* have one thing in common: the *kamiza*, or upper seat (also known as the *joza*). In accordance with ancient Shinto custom, the location of the *kamiza* is the same in every *kyudojo*. It is always placed at the very right of the *shajo* (looking outward), and everything else—the starting and shooting lines, the regular seating area, and the lower seat—is positioned in relation to it.

The *Shajo*

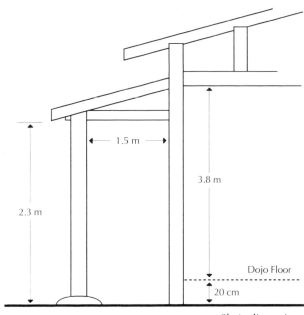

Shajo dimensions

Traditionally, the *kamiza* also housed a *kamidana*, a small Shinto altar, but because the postwar Japanese constitution requires the separation of church and state affairs, the *kamidana* is no longer included in public facilities. But even without a *kamidana*, the *kamiza* is a place deserving of great respect. It is the place where the teacher and guests of honor sit. Therefore, students should not enter the *kamiza* unless they are invited or have good reason to be there.

The *yamichi* is the open ground between the *shajo* and the target

The *Matoba*

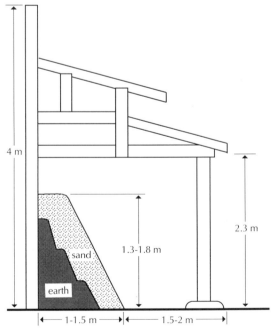

Matoba/Azuchi dimensions

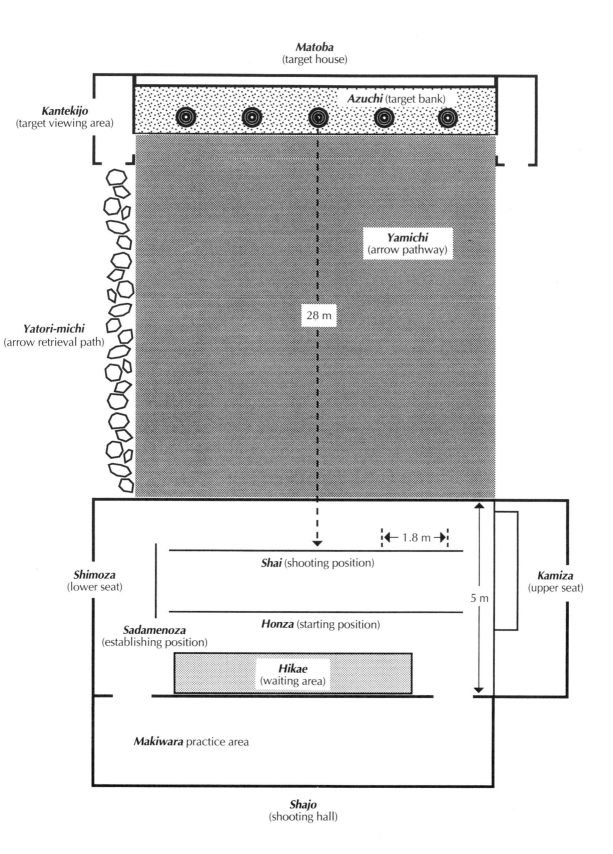

Matoba
(target house)

Kantekijo
(target viewing area)

Azuchi (target bank)

Yamichi
(arrow pathway)

28 m

Yatori-michi
(arrow retrieval path)

Shimoza
(lower seat)

1.8 m

Shai (shooting position)

Kamiza
(upper seat)

Honza (starting position)

5 m

Sadamenoza
(establishing position)

Hikae
(waiting area)

Makiwara practice area

Shajo
(shooting hall)

house. Normally, it is extremely simple in design: a neatly trimmed grass lawn or flat stretch of earth or sand, for example. Sometimes, though, the *yamichi* is designed with a creative touch and may include ornamental plants, rock formations, or even a shallow pond or stream. However, one must be careful not to get overly creative when designing the *yamichi* because arrows sometimes go astray and must be retrieved from its interior.

The *matoba* is a narrow, roofed structure that closely mimics the architectural style of the *shajo*. This part of the *kyudojo* is also called the *azuchi*. However, the *azuchi* is actually just the bank of sand that holds the targets, while the *matoba* is the structure that houses it.

The main function of the *matoba* is to protect the *azuchi* from the elements. At the very least, then, it will have supporting walls at the back and side and a roof that extends a meter or so beyond the *azuchi* face. Most of the time a narrow curtain called an *azuchi-maku* is hung from the eaves. It is more than just decorative since it keeps stray arrows from striking the hard back wall of the *matoba*. A well-designed *matoba* may also have a target storage room and an observation area for the target assistants. It might even be equipped with a set of shutters that enclose the *azuchi* when it is not in use.

The best *azuchi* are made of sifted river sand. Because of this, they require a great amount of upkeep. The slope of the sandbank is fairly steep—approximately twenty-five degrees—which means it must be watered, packed, and shaped with a flat trowel almost daily to keep it from collapsing. To add stability the sand is laid over a foundation of packed earth. If that is impractical, sand- or earth-filled bags can be used to build the foundation.

Sometimes the *azuchi* will collapse if the sand is of poor quality. If that is the case, sawdust can be added in a ratio of one part sawdust to four parts sand. Another technique is to periodically dampen the sand with salt water, this is especially useful in winter because it also helps to keep the *azuchi* from freezing. Neither method, however, is a substitute for proper care and maintenance of the *azuchi* area.

C H A P T E R
5

Equipment and Accessories

The Japanese Bow (*Yumi*)

Nowhere in the world is there a bow quite like the Japanese *yumi*. It is unique in every sense. It is exceptionally long, over two meters, and asymmetrical; the grip is positioned below center. And it is constructed today using the same techniques and the same simple materials—bamboo and wood—that were used more than 400 years ago. Unsurpassed in beauty and grace, the *yumi* embodies the spirit of Japan. It is simple and elegant, and deeply rooted in tradition. Throughout its history the *yumi* has been revered as much for its artistry as for its practical value.

The Evolution of the *Yumi*

The bows used by the early Japanese were of various lengths. The majority, however, were made in the short, center-gripped style common to most prehistoric cultures. As time passed, progressively longer bows appeared, and by the third century B.C. a bow nearly two meters in length had come into common use. This bow, the *maruki-yumi,* was made from a small sapling or tree limb (often catalpa wood) and had a centered grip. It was very similar to the bow currently used by the forest people of Malaysia and New Guinea. Thus it is thought that this bow was introduced to Japan from the cultures of the South Sea islands.

It is unknown when the Japanese first developed the asymmetrical bow, but archaeologists have found a *dotaku*, a bell-shaped bronze casting, dating back to the late Yayoi period (250 B.C. to A.D. 330), which depicts a hunter using what most archaeologists agree is an asymmetrical bow. The earliest written record of such a bow is in the *Gishi Wajin-den*, a section concerning Japan in the Wei Chronicle, a

PERIOD	BOW TYPE	CONSTRUCTION
Prehistoric	*Maruki*	One-piece sapling
9th–10th century	*Fusetake*	Two-piece wood and bamboo
12th century	*Sanmaeuchi*	Three-piece wood and bamboo
14th–15th century	*Shihodake*	Wood core surrounded by bamboo
Mid-16th century	*Sanbonhigo*	Three-piece bamboo laminate core surrounded by wood and bamboo
Early 17th century	*Yohonhigo*	Four-piece bamboo laminate core surrounded by wood and bamboo
Sometime after the 17th century	*Gohonhigo*	Five-piece bamboo or bamboo and wood laminate core surrounded by wood and bamboo

 *Azusa* (catalpa wood)  *Higo* (bamboo or bamboo and wood laminate)

Madake (bamboo)   *Haze* (waxwood)

Chinese history compiled in the third century. The chronicler describes the people of the Japanese islands as using "a wooden bow with upper and lower limbs of different lengths, and bamboo arrows with points of iron or bone." The oldest asymmetrical bow found to date was unearthed in Nara, and is estimated to have been made around the fifth century.

There has been much speculation about why the Japanese bow has a unique design. One source theorizes that it is because the lower grip made it easier to shoot the long bow from horseback. Unfortunately, this explanation does not take into account the fact that use of the

Asymmetrical bow depicted on a *dotaku* from the Yayoi period (250 B.C.- A.D.330)

asymmetrical bow probably predated mounted archery in Japan by several hundred years. However, it might explain why the design of the bow was never changed. A more popular theory is that since the original bow was made from a thin sapling, and because the base of the sapling was naturally thicker than the top, the grip was lowered to achieve a balanced draw. The only problem with this thinking is that even primitive man had the tools and know-how to shave the bow to a uniform thickness. Of course, the early bow maker might have preferred to cut a branch or sapling and leave it at that, but this does not explain why the grip was left off-center once more sophisticated bow-making techniques came into use. Still another explanation for the asymmetrical design of the Japanese bow is that the Yayoi archers highly prized bows of great length. An exceptionally long bow made quite an imposing weapon because it appeared a great deal more powerful than a shorter bow of comparable strength. But because of the small stature of the Yayoi people and the probable tendency for the Yayoi hunters to shoot from a crouched position, there was a practical limit to the length a center-gripped bow could be. Thus, as the length of their bows increased, the Yayoi archers had to lower the grip in order to be able to shoot effectively.

From the fourth to the ninth century, Chinese thought strongly influenced the Japanese court system. As a result, the Chinese bow—a short, center-gripped, composite bow made from horn, sinew, and wood—was introduced to Japan for use in court rituals. However, the Chinese bow failed to supplant the *yumi*. In truth, it wasn't long before the Japanese court nobles abandoned the Chinese bow and returned to the elegant simplicity of their native *yumi*. Even so, the sophisticated design of the Chinese bow impressed the Japanese bow makers. So much so, in fact, that they would eventually incorporate many of the same construction techniques into the design of the *yumi*.

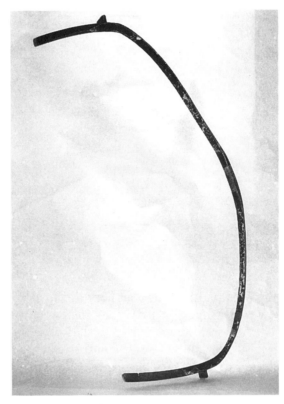

Early Chinese bow

During the Heian period (794-1185), the power of the samurai increased dramatically, and as might be expected, more time and effort went into the research and development of weapons. About this time, the length of the *yumi* was fixed at a little over two meters, and the laminate construction of the Chinese bow was adopted for the *yumi*. By the end of the tenth century the Japanese had developed a two-piece, bamboo and wood, laminated *yumi* (*fusetake*). This was followed by a three-piece *yumi* (*sanmaeuchi*), which came into use about the time of the Gempei War. Then, sometime around the fourteenth or fifteenth century, the *shihodake-yumi* appeared.

The *shihodake-yumi* was considered revolutionary in design. It was constructed of a single piece of wood surrounded by four strips of bamboo. This design led the way for further experimentation with cross-lamination techniques, and by the middle of the sixteenth century the *sanbonhigo-yumi* had been developed. This bow was constructed using a highly sophisticated lamination technique that incorporated vertical strips of bamboo and wood (*higo*), sandwiched between two horizontal lengths of bamboo. At this point, the *yumi* was regarded as being nearly perfect. So much so, in fact, that the design and construction of the Japanese *yumi* has remained relatively unchanged since that time. As a result, the bamboo *yumi* used in modern kyudo is practically identical to the ones used in the sixteenth and seventeenth centuries.

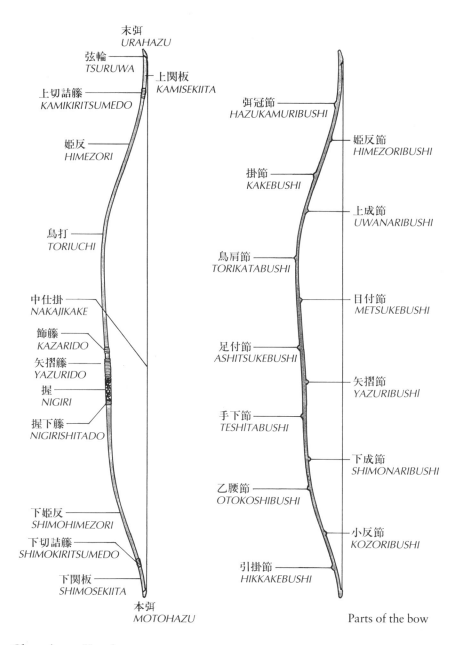

末弭
URAHAZU

弦輪
TSURUWA

上切詰籐
KAMIKIRITSUMEDO

上関板
KAMISEKIITA

姫反
HIMEZORI

鳥打
TORIUCHI

中仕掛
NAKAJIKAKE

節籐
KAZARIDO

矢摺籐
YAZURIDO

握
NIGIRI

握下籐
NIGIRISHITADO

下姫反
SHIMOHIMEZORI

下切詰籐
SHIMOKIRITSUMEDO

下関板
SHIMOSEKIITA

本弭
MOTOHAZU

弭冠節
HAZUKAMURIBUSHI

姫反節
HIMEZORIBUSHI

掛節
KAKEBUSHI

上成節
UWANARIBUSHI

鳥肩節
TORIKATABUSHI

目付節
METSUKEBUSHI

足付節
ASHITSUKEBUSHI

矢摺節
YAZURIBUSHI

手下節
TESHITABUSHI

下成節
SHIMONARIBUSHI

乙腰節
OTOKOSHIBUSHI

小反節
KOZORIBUSHI

引掛節
HIKKAKEBUSHI

Parts of the bow

Choosing a *Yumi*

Basically, there are three types of *yumi* used in modern kyudo: standard bamboo *yumi*, lacquered bamboo *yumi*, and *yumi* made from synthetic materials (fiberglass or carbon).

Because of their durability and low cost, synthetic *yumi* are most often used by schools or large kyudo clubs where there is an inordinately high number of beginners. They are also desirable in areas where the climate is too cold or dry to use a bamboo *yumi* safely. Aside from those special instances, however, synthetic materials should be avoided in the practice of kyudo. Practicing with them can

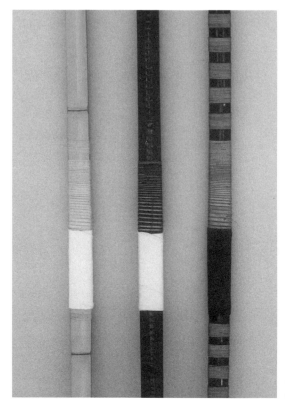

From left to right: *Take-yumi, urushi-yumi,* and *shigeto-yumi*

be likened to using plastic tableware at a formal dinner party. It will serve the same purpose as fine china but will greatly detract from the beauty and elegance of the event. It is not only a question of aesthetics, however. The nature of kyudo is such that it requires the warmth and sensitivity of natural materials to bring its hidden truths to the surface.

In the days of the samurai, bamboo *yumi* were usually covered with several layers of *urushi* (lacquer). This technique both strengthened the *yumi* and protected it from the elements. Often, the *yumi* was wrapped with parallel bands of fine thread before the lacquer was applied. The wrapping made it exceptionally durable, which is why most samurai preferred to take this type of *yumi* into battle. Sometimes a lacquered bow was wound with thin, rattanlike strips of wood in regular patterns. This type of bow is known as a *shigeto-yumi*. The *shigeto-yumi* was, and to this day is still, used only by archers of the highest caliber.

Urushi-yumi are made today by only a few select bow makers. Consequently, they are extremely expensive. Their cost, coupled with their comparatively heavy physical weight, makes them unsuitable for daily practice. These days the *urushi-yumi* is mostly reserved for formal shooting ceremonies.

The *yumi* of choice for most kyudo practitioners today is the standard bamboo *yumi*, or *take-yumi*. The simplicity and clean line of the *take-yumi* nicely complement the form and shooting procedure of modern kyudo.

Japanese *yumi* are measured in *shaku* and *sun*, the traditional Japanese measuring system. One *sun* is roughly equal to three centimeters, and ten *sun* equal one *shaku*. The normal length of a *yumi* is seven *shaku*, three *sun*, or about 221 centimeters. This length is ideal for people of average Japanese height (150-165 cm). But others, especially those who are exceptionally tall, should avoid using a normal-length *yumi* since there is a heightened chance of it breaking under the stress. To alleviate this problem, modern *yumi* are made in a variety of lengths: short (*tsumari*), normal (*namisun*), and long (*nobi*). The ideal length of one's *yumi* is determined by both height and *yazuka*, the length of one's arrow.

In addition to the different lengths, *yumi* are available in a variety of pull strengths, normally in the ten to thirty kilogram range. Most beginners start with a bow of ten or twelve kilograms then gradually increase the pull strength over a period of several months. It is very important to match the pull strength to the individual. It must be neither too light nor too strong. Naturally, pull strength varies from person to person, depending on his or her age, body type, and experience. The average pull strength for an experienced middle-aged male archer is around eighteen kilograms. The average for women is a few kilograms less.

However, before deciding on a pull strength it is important to know that bow makers use a ninety centimeter *yazuka* as the standard for determining a bow's strength. As a result, the actual pull strength will be greater when one's *yazuka* is longer than ninety centimeters—approximately one kilogram for every additional five centimeters of *yazuka*.

Choosing a *yumi* is not easy. Questions of type, length, strength,

ARCHER'S HEIGHT	ARCHER'S ARROW LENGTH	RECOMMENDED BOW LENGTH
Less than 150 cm	Less than 85 cm	*Sansun-tsumari* (212 cm)
150-165 cm	85-90 cm	*Namisun* (221 cm)
165-180 cm	90-100 cm	*Nisun-nobi* (227 cm)
180-195 cm	100-105 cm	*Yonsun-nobi* (233 cm)
195-205 cm	105-110 cm	*Rokusun-nobi* (239 cm)
More than 205 cm	More than 110 cm	*Hassun-nobi* (245 cm)

maker, and cost must all be considered. Novice practitioners are advised to purchase a *yumi* of moderate cost at first. Then later, once their technique improves and they are less likely to damage their equipment, they can move up to a more expensive *yumi*.

Caring for the *Yumi*

A good bamboo *yumi* seems almost alive. When new, it is strong and full of energy, and it must be watched over carefully and gently corrected to keep it in proper shape. With maturity it will settle down and require less attention, but it will also get "tired" more easily and need more rest. In old age it will be set in its ways and will have lost much of its strength, but if treated with respect it will respond in a way that no new *yumi* can.

Every *yumi* has its own distinct personality. It is no wonder, given all the variables that go into its creation: bamboo quality, bonding agents (natural or synthetic), construction techniques, and the personal touches of the bow maker, just to name a few. That is why it is not easy to establish a single set of rules for maintaining the condition of the *yumi*. Still, certain guidelines do exist and if they are closely followed a *yumi* will last for several generations.

A bamboo *yumi* is not especially delicate. However, it is vulnerable to extreme cold, moisture, dryness, or neglect. The great Japanese bow maker Higo Saburo (Matsunaga Shigeji) recommends that we treat a *yumi* as we would treat ourselves. When the weather is cold, warm the *yumi* by rubbing it with a silk cloth or chamois. In humid conditions the *yumi* should be dried with a soft towel. If the air is dry the *yumi* should be wiped down periodically with a moistened cloth and then dried with a towel.

Correcting the Shape of the *Yumi*

Perhaps the greatest threat to a *yumi* is neglect. A bamboo *yumi*, especially a new bamboo *yumi*, will sometimes lose its shape if left unattended for long periods of time. The problem lessens as the *yumi* matures but it is rare to find a bamboo *yumi* that does not need a little reshaping from time to time. Naturally, an extremely warped *yumi* should only be repaired by a professional who may have to use heat or shaping forms to restore the *yumi* to its proper shape. However, before it reaches that point the shape of a *yumi* can be corrected by applying gentle pressure against the affected joints.

When looking down the line of the string, the shape of the *yumi* is such that the string is set slightly to the right of center (*iriki*). When the string is left of center (*deki*) or extremely *iriki*, a shaping block can be attached for a few days to return the *yumi* to its correct shape.

It is also important to check the shape of an unstrung *yumi* from time to time. Ideally, it should have a curvature height of between twelve and twenty centimeters. Anything less usually means that the

Master Bow Maker Higo Saburo

Higo Saburo (Matsunaga Shigeji and his son, Shigemasa)

yumi is tired and overused. Therefore, it should be left to rest unstrung for a while. On the other hand, an excessively curved *yumi* should be kept strung until it returns to its proper shape. One should be especially careful when using an excessively curved *yumi* since it is more likely to throw the string or twist upon release.

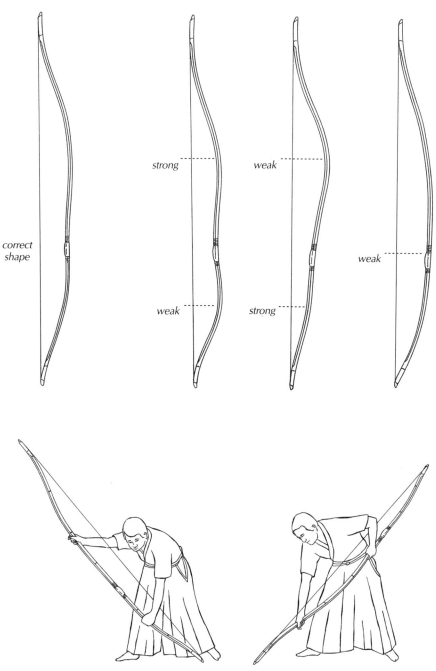

Correcting the shape of a *yumi* with hand pressure

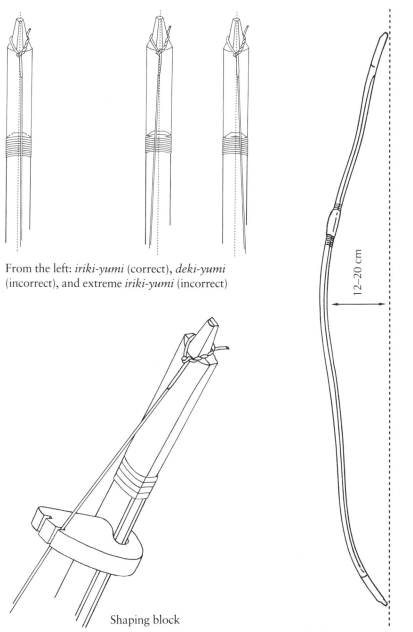

From the left: *iriki-yumi* (correct), *deki-yumi* (incorrect), and extreme *iriki-yumi* (incorrect)

Shaping block

Correct height for an unstrung *yumi*

12–20 cm

The Bowstring (*Tsuru*)

Basically there are three types of *tsuru*: natural, synthetic, and a mixture of the two. The best *tsuru* are made from natural hemp (*asa*). They provide the smoothest release and the finest *tsurune* (string sound). However, they are not very durable—particularly in dry conditions. Synthetic or mixed *tsuru* are stronger but they obviously lack the quality and elegance of natural strings. Choice of a *tsuru*, then, is up to the individual who must decide which type of *tsuru* best suits his or her own needs and shooting habits.

Tsuru come in lengths that correspond to that of the *yumi* (*namisun*, *nisun-nobi*, etc.) They also come in different weights (*momei*), and range from 1.6 *momei* (six grams) to 2.4 *momei* (nine grams). As a general rule the lighter strings are used in the summer or on *yumi* with a light pull strength, while the heavier strings are best used in winter or on heavier *yumi*.

Tsuru are coated with *kusune*, a pine resin and oil mixture that binds the fibers and strengthens the string. It is generally a good idea to strengthen the *tsuru* before and after each practice session with a woven hemp pad called a *waraji*. To do this, fold the *waraji* over the string and vigorously rub it up and down the length of the string. The rubbing action melts the *kusune* and rebinds any loosened threads, thereby considerably increasing the life of the *tsuru*.

Spare *tsuru* should be stored where they are protected from excessive moisture or dryness. Most archers also keep one or two fully prepared strings in a *tsurumaki*, a circular string holder made out of rattan or wood. The *tsurumaki* is either carried on the archer's person or kept close at hand in the event that a string should break during shooting.

Tsurumaki (above) and *waraji*

Tying the *Tsuru*

When you purchase a new *tsuru*, you will find the *tsuruwa* (loop) tied only at the lower end. It is necessary, therefore, to tie the upper *tsuruwa* yourself. Normally, the upper part of the *tsuru* is covered with red cloth and the loop is begun about two or three centimeters above the point where the red cloth meets the string fibers. But because every *yumi* and *tsuru* varies slightly in length, it is best to make a quick measurement prior to tying the loop. The easiest way to do this is to place the lower loop over the upper nock (*urahazu*) of the *yumi* and bend the *yumi* as if you were actually stringing it. Stretch the *tsuru* and mark the point where the red cloth meets the base of the bottom nock (*motohazu*). Remove the *tsuru* and, starting from the point you marked, follow the sequence of drawings below to finish tying the *tsuruwa*.

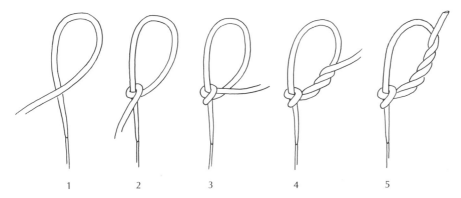

Tying the *tsuruwa*

Stringing the *Yumi*

To string the *yumi* place the red *tsuruwa* over the *urahazu* (the twisted portion should be on the right side.) Place the *urahazu* in the pocket of a stringing block or anchor it against a piece of wood. Hold the bottom loop of the *tsuru* between your lips and place your left hand on the grip. Do not push down on the grip. Using your left hand as a brace, lift the bottom of the *yumi* a few centimeters and set it on your left thigh. Take the lower end of the *tsuru* in your right hand and rotate it clockwise two or three times to take up the slack. Place the bottom loop at the base of the *motohazu* and gently lean into the grip until the loop slips over the end of the *motohazu* (the twisted portion should be on the left side.) The distance between the *tsuru* and the grip should be about fifteen centimeters once the bow has been strung. If not, check the shape of the *yumi* or retie the *tsuru*.

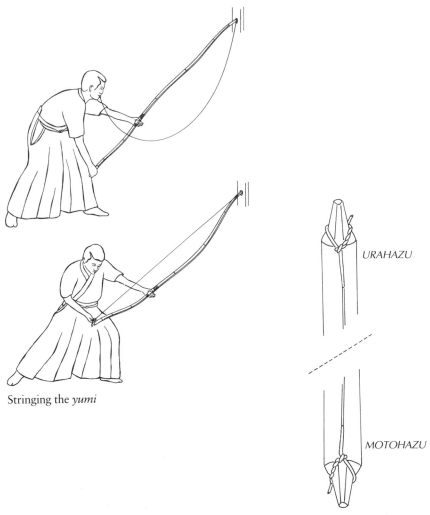

Stringing the *yumi*

URAHAZU

MOTOHAZU

Position of the string on the *yumi*

Preparing the Nocking Area (*Nakajikake*)

Once the yumi is strung the *nakajikake* must be prepared before the arrow can be nocked. The *nakajikake* is made from a short piece—about twelve centimeters—of loose hemp. Using the piece of hemp, measure from a point about two centimeters above the grip directly across to the *tsuru* and mark the spot with a pencil. Rub the nocking area with the *waraji* to strengthen the *tsuru*, then coat the area with *kusune* or common white glue. Flatten the piece of hemp and, working from the point you marked, wrap a short section of it downward around the string from right to left. If necessary, add a bit more glue and tightly wind the remainder of the hemp downward in the opposite direction. To finish, vigorously rub two wooden blocks back and forth over the *nakajikake* to tighten the binding.

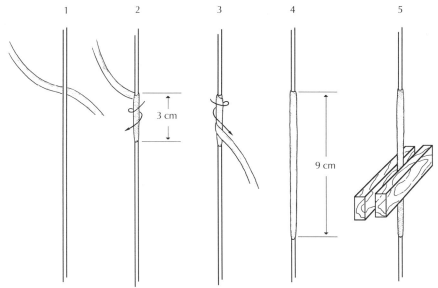

Preparing the *nakajikake*

Storing the *Yumi*

When not in use, a *yumi* should be stored in a cloth wrap to protect it from nicks and scratches. Leather or vinyl covers are useful for transporting a *yumi* in bad weather but it should not be kept in these materials for extended periods since they can trap excessive moisture which is harmful to the *yumi*. Ideally, unstrung *yumi* should be stored horizontally. When this is impractical they can be stored upright on the same vertical stands used for daily practice. Remember, a bamboo *yumi* is most vulnerable in extremely wet or dry conditions so be sure not to store it in a damp basement or next to a heater.

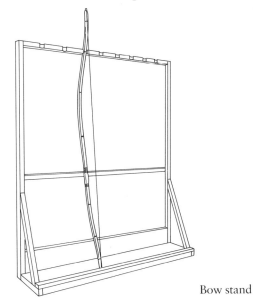

Bow stand

The Arrows (*Ya*)

Japanese arrows are quite unlike their Western counterparts. They are extremely long, close to a meter or more, with feathers about fifteen centimeters in length. Like the *yumi*, they are made today in much the same way as they were in the past, with all natural materials—with the exception of the iron points, of course. The shafts are made out of *yadake*, a slender, very durable variety of bamboo. The nocks are normally carved out of horn or bamboo. And the feathers come from eagles, hawks, or other large birds.

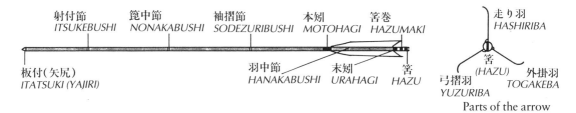

射付節 ITSUKEBUSHI　　箆中節 NONAKABUSHI　　袖摺節 SODEZURIBUSHI　　本矧 MOTOHAGI　　筈巻 HAZUMAKI　　走り羽 HASHIRIBA

板付(矢尻) ITATSUKI (YAJIRI)　　羽中節 HANAKABUSHI　　末矧 URAHAGI　　筈 HAZU　　弓摺羽 YUZURIBA　　筈 (HAZU)　　外掛羽 TOGAKEBA

Parts of the arrow

The Arrow Shaft (*No*)

Classical *ya* had different-shaped shafts for different purposes: barrelled shafts (*mugi-tsubu*) for long-distance shooting and tapered shafts (*suginari*) for more accuracy at close range. Most modern *ya* have shafts that are either straight (*ichimonji*) or only slightly tapered (*ko-suginari*).

Bamboo shafts also come in different thicknesses, weighing anywhere from 5 *momei* (18.7 grams) to 7.5 *momei* (28 grams). The lighter arrows generally fly faster, but they lose their stability when shot from a stronger bow. When choosing the diameter of their arrows, most archers also take into account the length of the arrow as well as body size in order to achieve an aesthetically pleasing balance between body and equipment. One's *yazuka*, or arrow length, is determined by measuring from the center of the throat to the tip of the outstretched left arm, and adding an extra five centimeters for safety.

In recent years, aluminum or carbon-fiber shafts have come into use. But even though they, too, are fitted with real feathers, they cannot compare with the natural beauty and feel of bamboo arrows.

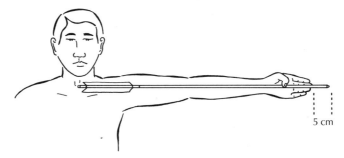

5 cm

Determining the *yazuka*

The Arrowhead (*Yajiri/Yanone*)

Classical arrowheads, or *yajiri,* ranged from simple tips of iron used for hunting or war to elaborately crafted ceremonial broad heads. Today, with the exception of special ceremonial procedures, these arrowheads are no longer used.

Modern points (*yanone*) come in two types: regular target points and *makiwara* points. Most metal points fit over the end of the arrow shaft, and are available in a variety of diameters which enable them to be attached to the shaft without the use of any bonding agents. In cases where the point is not quite large enough to fit over the shaft, the end of the shaft can be shaved down a little to ensure a proper fit.

Metal *makiwara* points are fine for daily practice but better *makiwara-ya,* like those used for ceremonial purposes, are fitted with horn points. These points are first inserted into the open end of the shaft, secured by a little *kusune* or common white glue, then shaped with a file or knife to create an arrow with a smooth, clean line.

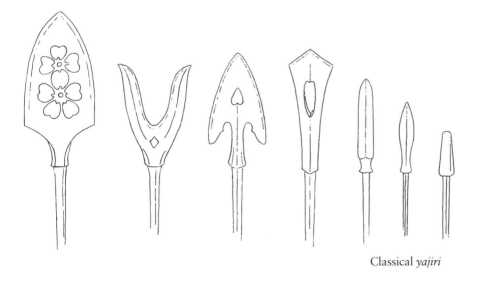

Classical *yajiri*

Target point   *Makiwara* point

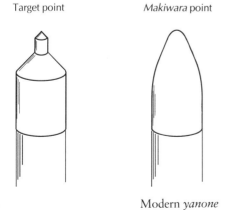

Modern *yanone*

The Nock (*Hazu*)

The great majority of nocks today are made from goat or deer horn. Like the horn *makiwara* points, they are inserted into the arrow shaft and, if necessary, filed down to match its diameter. Most of the time the nocking slot of a horn *hazu* has to be finished by the archer so that it will correctly fit the nocking area of his *tsuru*. To do this use a small flat file and a very thin rattail file to make the inner portion of the slot slightly wider than the upper part. The resulting keyhole-like shape keeps the arrow firmly secured to the string.

Many older *ya*, and some ceremonial *ya*, have bamboo nocks. Often this type of nock is carved directly from the end of the arrow shaft. Sometimes, though, a bamboo nock is fashioned from a separate piece of bamboo and set into the end of the shaft, thus allowing the nock to be replaced if it breaks or is damaged in any way.

The Feathers (*Hane*)

Without a doubt the most impressive, and quite often the most expensive, part of an arrow is the feathers. The finest feathers, both in terms of beauty and durability, come from large birds of prey; most notably northern sea eagles (*otori*) and hawks (*taka*). Both of these birds are getting more and more difficult to find in the wild, however. Indeed, the sea eagle has become so rare that it is now protected by an international agreement. Consequently, sea eagle feathers are no longer collected. Today, most feathers come from lesser eagles, geese, swans, and even turkeys—any of the larger birds that are not endangered.

Feather quality varies greatly with the type of bird and the kind of feather. The very best are the *ishiuchi*, the outermost tail feathers of an eagle or hawk. Next come the inner tail feathers (*oba*), and finally the wing feathers (*teba*). In the case of other birds like turkeys or swans, only the wing feathers are used. These feathers are relatively inexpensive. However, they do not hold up under repeated use as well as eagle or hawk feathers.

Feathers from both the right side and the left side are used to make arrows. Arrows that have feathers that curve to the left are called *haya*, or first arrows, while those that curve to the right are called *otoya*, or second arrows. In the normal kyudo shooting procedure, two arrows are shot in succession—the *haya*, and then the *otoya*.

Care and Storage of the Arrows

After each practice session one should, at the very least, wipe the arrows clean with a dry cloth. It is also a good idea to periodically oil the shafts with either walnut or camellia oil. This is especially important if the arrows are to be stored for a long time. It is the feathers, however, that need the most care. After each shooting they should be gently pulled back into shape to keep them from bending or breaking. If the feathers get to the point where shaping by hand is no longer effective, they can be lightly steamed until they regain their shape.

Arrows should always be stored vertically to avoid crushing the feathers. The most commonly used storage case these days is the *yazutsu*, a long, tubelike container designed to hold about six to eight arrows. Larger collections are stored in open stands or racks, or in arrow cases made of glass and wood.

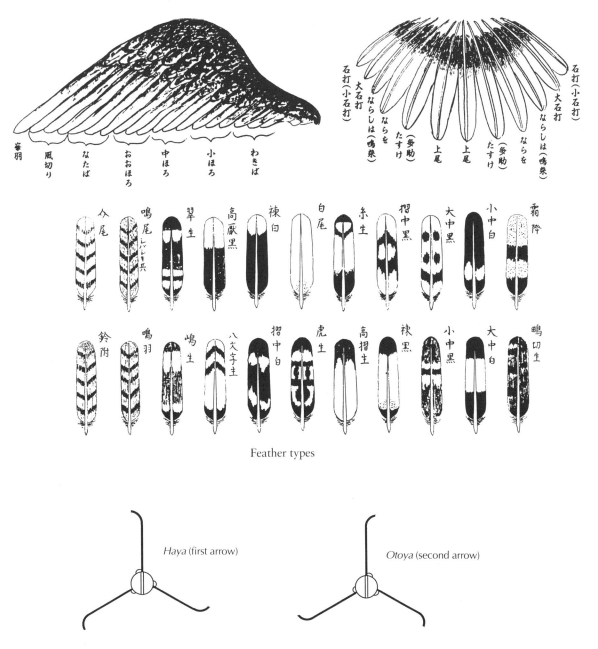

Feather types

Haya (first arrow)

Otoya (second arrow)

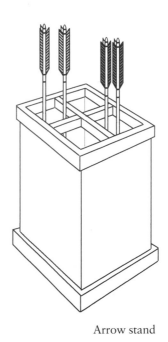

Arrow stand

The *yazutsu*

The Glove (*Yugake*)

In the early days of Japanese archery the bow was pulled with the thumb and forefinger in the so-called "pinch style" familiar to every child who has ever played with a bow and arrow. Around the seventh century, the Japanese adopted the northern Chinese style of pulling the bow with the thumb. The Chinese used a thumb ring made of horn or stone to pull the string. It is doubtful, however, that the Japanese ever used such a ring, preferring instead to use a leather band. Eventually a full glove was used, but aside from a slightly reinforced inner thumb there was nothing particularly special about this glove since the archer also had to be able to use his sword or ride while wearing it.

Gloves like the ones used today, with a hardened thumb and wrist, appeared after the Onin Wars (1467–1477) had ended and the emphasis turned to target shooting. These gloves are made of deerskin with a horn or wood thumb insert. This design greatly increases the archer's ability to hold the draw for an extended length of time, allowing him to more closely study the relationship between himself and his shooting.

From the right: Ishizu Shigesada (*yumishi*), Onuma Hogetsu (*kakeshi*), Ishizu Iwao (*yashi*), Kato Zenbei (*kakeshi*), and Watanabe Rikiyo (*yashi*)

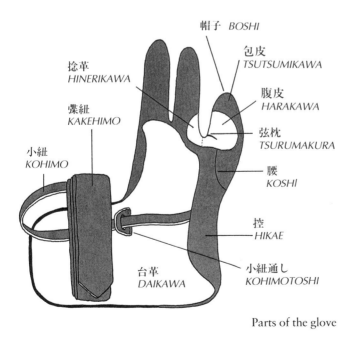

Parts of the glove

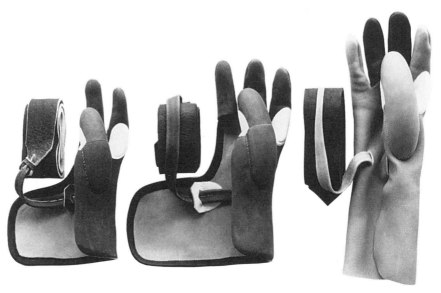

From the left: *mitsugake*, *yotsugake*, and *morogake*

There are basically three types of *yugake* in use today: *mitsugake* (three-finger gloves), *yotsugake* (four-finger gloves), and *morogake* (five-finger gloves). These gloves are all right-handed because Japanese archers always face the *kamiza* when shooting. Aside from the number of fingers, there are subtle differences in how the gloves are made. The thumb of a *yotsugake,* for example, is set at a slightly lower angle than that of a *mitsugake.* Consequently, certain schools or teachers will prefer one glove type over the others. The *morogake*, for instance, is used almost exclusively by practitioners of Ogasawara Ryu, while the exponents of Heki Ryu prefer to use the *mitsugake* when shooting at close range. The *yotsugake,* on the other hand, was originally designed and used for the long-distance shooting competition at Kyoto's Sanjusangendo. Today, however, many advanced practitioners prefer to use the *yotsugake* for close-range shooting because it takes less effort to draw and hold the bow with a *yotsugake*.

Tying the *Yugake*

Working from a seated position, lay your hand, palm up, on the right thigh and wrap the small band around the wrist so that it fits in the hollow between the base of the hand and the wrist bone. Continue wrapping the large strap around the wrist, leaving a fifteen-centimeter length at the end. Moving from the base of the hand, tuck the end piece under the top layer of the large strap and pull it toward you. Slightly tighten the strap layers and loop the end piece over and through the top strap once again. To finish, tighten the strap layers and straighten the loop.

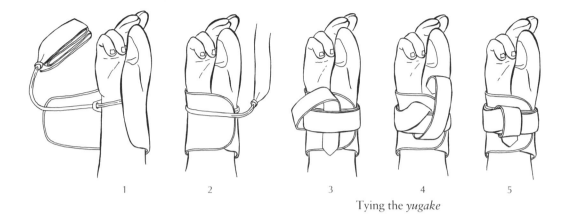

Tying the *yugake*

Caring for the *Yugake*

In Japan it is not unusual to find someone using a glove that once belonged to a parent or grandparent. With proper care a good *yugake* should last for decades.

When new, a *yugake* is naturally stiff and needs to be broken in a little before it can be used properly. To do this, one should try on the glove and alternately fold and stretch the fingers to soften the leather. The wrist area should also be gently worked, but care must be taken not to break the stiffened leather piece that is attached to the thumb.

It is important to protect the glove from moisture. After practice, both the *yugake* and the cotton underglove that is worn with it should be left to dry if they have become dampened by perspiration. Only then should they be stored away in a cloth or leather glove-bag. As an extra precaution some archers add a small packet of desiccant to protect the glove from mildew. This is a good preventative measure, especially when the humidity is high, but care should be taken to keep the package of desiccant away from the *yugake* itself lest it stain the deerskin. Dirt can be cleaned from a *yugake* with a soft gum eraser. The eraser is particularly useful for removing any accumulated *giriko*, the glove rosin that is rubbed over the thumb of the glove to keep the fingers from slipping off. In extreme cases a moist cloth can be used to clean the glove but solvents or harsh soaps should never be used since they can easily stain or damage the deerskin.

The Target (*Mato*)

There are a variety of targets used in kyudo today. They range in size from the tiny, nine-centimeter gold-foil *mato*, which is used on special occasions, to the 150-centimeter *mato* used in long-distance shooting (*enteki*). The most common target, however, is the thirty-six-centimeter *mato* used in *kinteki*, regular close-range shooting. The *kinteki* target is made of a circular wooden frame called a *matowaku*, and a paper target face. To prepare the target, use a mixture of water and

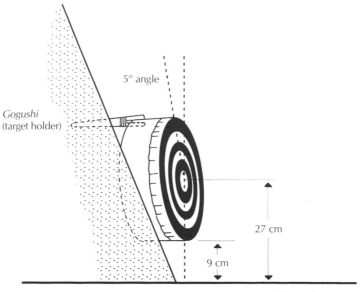

5° angle

Gogushi
(target holder)

27 cm

9 cm

Mato placement

ordinary paper glue to attach a plain piece of paper to the back of the target face. Apply another coat of the water and glue mixture to both sides of the target face and stretch it over the *matowaku*. Smooth and trim the edges of the paper and set the target in the sun to dry. The *mato* is then wedged into the target bank (*azuchi*) at a five-degree angle so that the center is twenty-seven centimeters above the ground. If desired, a wooden target holder (*gogushi*) can be used to support the top of the target.

The two target faces used most often in a regular *kyudojo* are the *kasumi-mato* (mist target) and the *hoshi-mato* (star target). The *kasumi-mato* has a series of concentric black circles of varied width, and the *hoshi-mato* has one black center circle. Aside from kyudo tests, where the *kasumi-mato* is the official standard, there are no rules governing the use of these targets in kyudo. Most *kyudojo*, however, use the *kasumi-mato* in daily practice and reserve the *hoshi-mato* for special training sessions.

First-time visitors to a *kyudojo* are usually surprised at how low the *mato* is positioned on the target bank. One possible explanation is that samurai archers shot from both kneeling and standing positions, with those kneeling taking up the front-line attack at close range. If the defending archers fired their arrows at chest height, only the standing archers would be hit, allowing the front lines to move unimpeded. Therefore, samurai archers initially concentrated their attack on the crouched warriors to thwart their advance.

Today the target is kept low partially out of tradition but there is another, more practical reason: Given the average height of the Japanese archer and the average pull strength of his bow, the target's

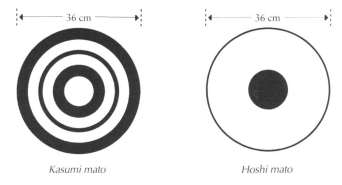

Kasumi mato   Hoshi mato

Two *mato* types

position allows the archer to keep his body symmetrical and his arrow horizontal when shooting from the normal *kinteki* distance of twenty-eight meters, thereby preserving the delicate aesthetics of modern kyudo.

The Practice Uniform (*Keiko-gi*)

To see an experienced archer shoot in formal *kimono* and *hakama*—classical Japanese attire—is to see kyudo at its most beautiful. Unfortunately, a good *kimono* is very expensive, often costing a thousand dollars or more. Consequently, most people only wear *kimono* on special occasions.

The standard practice uniform consists of a *kimono*-like top (*kyudo-gi*), a divided skirt (*hakama*), split-toed socks (*tabi*), and a cloth belt (*obi*). Women also wear a leather chest protector (*muneate*). There are some subtle differences in the uniforms worn by men and women. A man's *hakama*, for example, has a stiffened back piece that the woman's *hakama* does not have. This is because women traditionally wear their *hakama* higher on the waist than men do.

In Japan, the Zen Nihon Kyudo Renmei requires that all archers testing up to fifth *dan* wear a white *kyudo-gi* and white *tabi*. Men must wear a black *hakama*, while women are permitted to wear either black or navy-blue *hakama*. Archers testing above fifth *dan* are required to wear a *kimono* and *hakama*, along with white *tabi*. For the sake of simplicity, most *kyudojo* have their members follow the same standards for daily practice, but give higher-ranked members the option of wearing either the white *kyudo-gi* or a *kimono*.

At all times the kyudo uniform must be kept immaculately clean and neatly pressed. Nothing spoils the beauty of kyudo more than a person who is dirty and unkempt. Most *kyudo-gi* are made of cotton or synthetic materials and can be easily washed and ironed. *Hakama* should be carefully folded after each use to keep them neat and pressed. All this may seem trivial, but if a person does not even have the patience and discipline to keep a *keiko-gi* neat and clean, how can he or she ever expect to cope with the far greater demands that the practice of kyudo is sure to make.

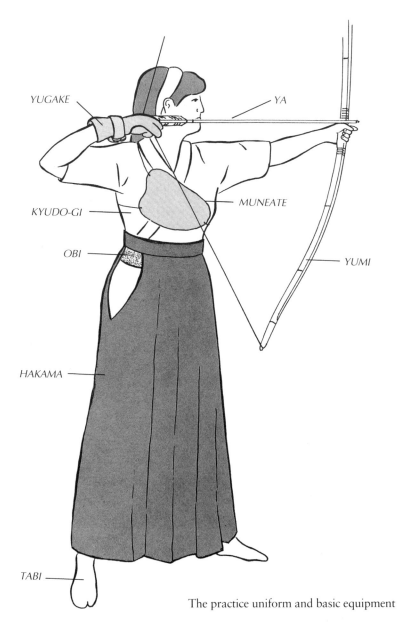

The practice uniform and basic equipment

Tying the *Obi*

Before tying the *obi* make sure that the *kyudo-gi* or *kimono* is put on correctly with the left side folded over the right. Working from the front, fold a thirty-centimeter section of one end of the *obi* in half lengthwise. Hold this end against your lower left side and wrap the *obi* from left to right around your waist, leaving a thirty-centimeter section at the end (if the *obi* is too long fold the end piece back). Wrap the wide end around the narrow end and pull it upward, tightening the *obi*. Fold the end of the wide section inward to form a "V" shape, then thread the narrow end through the "V" and pull it tight. Finish by turning the *obi* around to the right until the knot is in line with the center of the back.

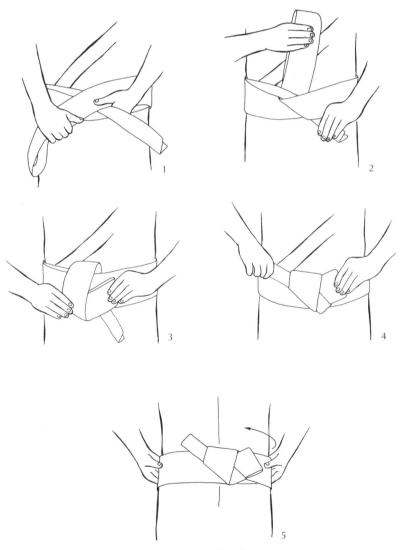

Tying the *obi*

Tying the *Hakama*

Hold the front of the *hakama* at the waist, then take the long ties on the sides around to the back. Cross the ties over the top of the *obi* knot and continue around and down to the front, crossing the left tie over the right. At a point just left of center, fold the right tie up, flat against the other tie, and continue both ties around to the back. Tie them in a bow beneath the *obi*. Pick up the back of the *hakama* and lay the back piece above the *obi* knot. Bring the back ties around and down to the front and cross them, left over right, at the center of the body. For women, the ties are then wrapped around to the back inside the *hakama* and tied in a bow under the *obi*. For men, the ties are tied in a simple square knot and the remainder of the tie is tucked beneath the *obi* on the left and right sides.

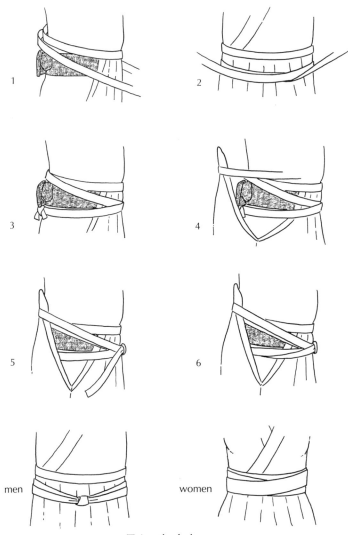

Tying the *hakama*

CHAPTER
6

Hassetsu: *The Eight Stages of Shooting*

The study of kyudo is divided into eight fundamental stages known as the *hassetsu*. The *hassetsu* reflect the knowledge and teaching experience of past generations of master archers and are the easiest, most efficient way to learn kyudo technique and shooting procedure.

It is important to understand that the *hassetsu* are presented here as separate actions only for the purpose of study. In truth, they are part of one continuous action and must be performed with seamless integration. That does not mean, however, that the movements of the *hassetsu* continue nonstop from beginning to end. There are, of course, moments in which the archer must pause in the shooting procedure. It is the spirit that never stops. It flows smooth and constant; starting even before the movements have begun and continuing well after the shooting has finished.

A popular saying in kyudo is "Shooting should be like flowing water." And if we take a moving stream as an example, we find that when we watch the ripples they appear to move separately from the rest of the water. They seem so only because we have focused our attention on them. However, if we step back and look at the water from a different perspective, the ripples merge into the whole of the stream. And so it is with kyudo. The *hassetsu* are there, like the ripples in the stream, but during the shooting they merge with the flow of the spirit.

Before studying the *hassetsu*, one should know that kyudo has developed along the following two lines: *bushakei*, the shooting style of the foot soldier, and *kishakei*, the style of the mounted archer. The styles differ in part because of the technique used to remove the arrow from its quiver and nock it to the string. Today, *kishakei* is more commonly called *reishakei*, or ceremonial-style shooting, because of its close association with Ogasawara Ryu ceremonial archery. Since the *hassetsu* are derived from the teachings of past masters of both styles, either *bushakei* or *reishakei* can be used when practicing the standard shooting procedure. One should be careful, however, not to mix elements of the two styles when shooting.

Ashibumi (footing)

Ashibumi is the foundation upon which the remaining stages of the *hassetsu* are built. Without firm, stable footing good shooting is virtually impossible. It is imperative, then, that you develop a thorough understanding of *ashibumi*.

Ashibumi

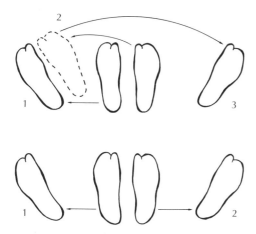

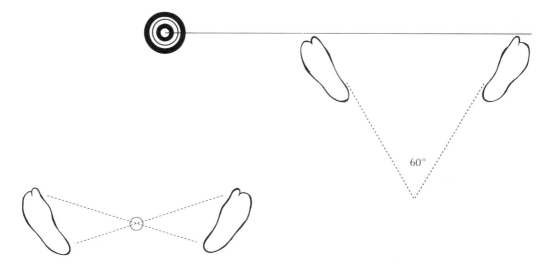

Two ways of making *ashibumi*: *reishakei* (above) and *bushakei*

Angle and alignment of the feet (right), and weight distribution.

There are two ways to position the feet when making *ashibumi*: the step and slide method used in *reishakei* and the two-step method used in *bushakei*. In both cases it is important to keep the body erect and to let the feet glide smoothly over the floor to avoid bobbing or swaying. As a rule, the feet are spread the distance of one's arrow length (*yazuka*) with the big toes in line with the center of the target. The angle of the footing should be sixty degrees, and the weight of the body should be evenly distributed so that the center of gravity is maintained between both feet. Equal pressure should be applied to both legs, and the knees should be stretched naturally. The feet must be set firmly on the ground, but you must be careful not to "plant" your feet or press excessively against the floor. Instead, you should feel as if the energy of the earth itself were rising up through the floor and into your legs and upper body. The bow and arrows are held at hip level with the bow on the left and the arrows on the right. Both elbows should point outward. The top of the bow is kept in line with the center of the body and held about ten centimeters above the floor. In *reishakei* the arrows are held so that the points protrude about ten centimeters from the glove. In *bushakei* only the ends of the points are exposed. In either case, the arrows are held at the same angle as the bow to form an imaginary triangle in front of you.

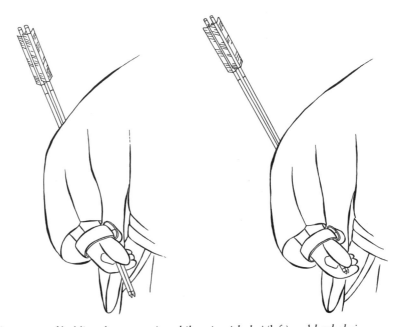

Two ways of holding the arrows in *ashibumi*: *reishakei* (left) and *bushakei*

Dozukuri (correcting the posture)

Once the feet are in place you must turn your attention to the posture of the upper body. Special care must be taken with the so-called three-cross relationship, where the shoulders, hips, and feet are held in line with one another, parallel to the floor. For this posture to work correctly, the shoulders must be kept down as the spine and back of the neck are gently stretched. The first arrow (*haya*) is knocked and held in place with the left forefinger, while the second arrow (*otoya*) is held beneath the *haya* between the ring and little fingers (*reishakei*), or between the middle and ring fingers (*bushakei*). The bottom end of the bow is rested on the left knee, and the bow is held so that the upper curve is in line with the center of the body. As the right hand is placed on the right hip you must correct your posture, taking care not to lean forward or backward, nor to the left or right. Then, depending on the type of glove used, the *otoya* is grasped and held at your right side in one of the two ways illustrated. The eyes look softly along the line of the nose to a point on the floor about four meters away. At this point you should regulate your breathing and let your weight settle naturally as you calm your mind and send your spirit forth in every direction, creating what is known in kyudo as *enso*, a feeling of roundness. As a final preparation do *tsurushirabe*, the inspection of the string, by first looking down the string then along the length of the arrow to the target. After a brief moment return your gaze to the nocking area and prepare to do *yugamae*.

Dozukuri

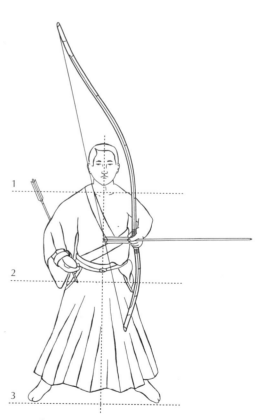

Three-cross relationship

Two ways of holding the *haya* and *otoya* in *dozukuri*: *reishakei* (left) and *bushakei*

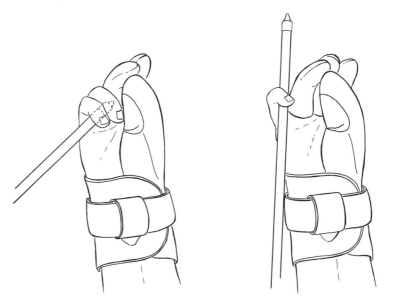

Two ways of holding the *otoya* in *dozukuri*: with three-fingered glove (left) and with four-fingered glove

Yugamae (readying the bow)

There are two styles of *yugamae* in modern kyudo. In the first, called *shomen no kamae*, the bow is kept in front of the body. In the second, called *shamen no kamae*, the bow is held off to the left side. Both ways include a series of preparatory movements known as *torikake* (setting the glove), *tenouchi* (gripping the bow), and *monomi* (viewing the target).

Yugamae

Shomen no kamae

Shamen no kamae

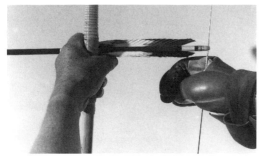 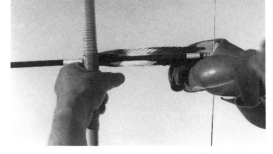

Torikake (part I)   *Torikake* (part II)

Torikake

One of the more difficult tasks in kyudo is learning how to make a clean, effortless release of the arrow. The ability to do this depends partly on one's ability to set the glove to the string in a correct manner.

To make *torikake*, first set the string in the nocking groove at the base of the thumb, then, depending on whether it is a three- or four-finger glove, lay the first two or the first three fingers across the thumb. Next, slide your thumb up the string until it meets the arrow.

There are four points that must be carefully considered when making *torikake*. First, you must be sure to set the thumb of the glove perpendicular to the string. Next, you must keep your wrist straight so that your forearm is in line with the thumb. Also, the thumb itself must be kept straight inside the glove, and never "hooked" or pressed against the sides. Finally, the right forearm must be rotated slightly. This pushes the arrow against the bow and keeps it in place during shooting.

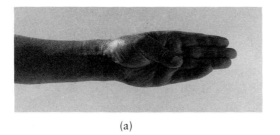 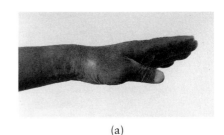

(a)   (a)

(b)   (b)

Making the *tenouchi*

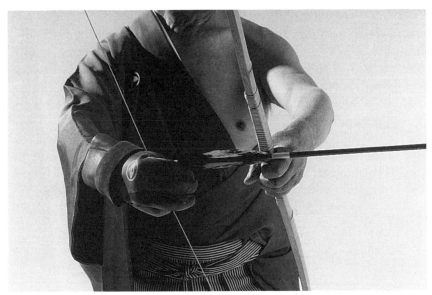

Torikake and *tenouchi* in *yugamae*

Tenouchi

After setting the glove you must prepare the *tenouchi,* a special method of holding the bow peculiar to Japanese archery. The importance of a correct *tenouchi* cannot be overemphasized. The flight and speed of the arrow is impossible to control if the *tenouchi* is not done properly. Also, the *yugaeri*—the action where, at the moment of release, the bow turns in place and the string swings around to the left—will not occur if the *tenouchi* is incorrect.

While a good *tenouchi* often takes years to develop, the basic technique is actually quite simple: Just keep the hand straight with the fingers extended and held close together, then fold the last three fingers in to meet the thumb. Particular attention must be paid to the correct alignment of the hand, wrist, and arm, and to the connection between the thumb and middle finger. Also, the open space between the bow and the base of the thumb must be maintained at all times. With careful practice these elements will lead to a well-prepared and properly executed *tenouchi.*

Monomi

Monomi, which literally means to view the object, is the final preparation in *yugamae.* In *monomi* you look at the target with calm, half-closed eyes. You should not think of aiming—*monomi* is not an aiming technique—you should simply send forth your spirit to make contact with the target. And from this moment on you must neither blink nor avert your gaze from the target lest you lose this vital connection.

Uchiokoshi (raising the bow)

In *uchiokoshi* you prepare to shoot by letting your spirit travel to the ends of your bow and arrows so that they become like extensions of your body. You then raise the bow in either of two ways: *shomen uchiokoshi*, where the bow is raised straight up in front of your body, or *shamen uchiokoshi*, where the bow is raised from the left-sided *shamen* position.

The bow must be lifted without force, like smoke rising into the air. And in the case of *shomen uchiokoshi*, it must be kept perfectly straight with the arrow held parallel to the floor. Normally, the bow is raised to a point where the hands are just above the head and the arms

Uchiokoshi   (a)

are at a forty-five degree angle, although this may vary somewhat depending on the person's physical condition. When raising the bow it is important to keep the arms and chest relaxed and the shoulders forward. This posture is often said to be like holding a large tree trunk. One must not take this teaching too literally, however, lest the arms appear unnaturally round.

The bow is raised in concert with the inhalation of the breath. At the peak of the move there is a short pause as the breath is softly exhaled. Then the archer inhales once more as he starts the drawing sequence.

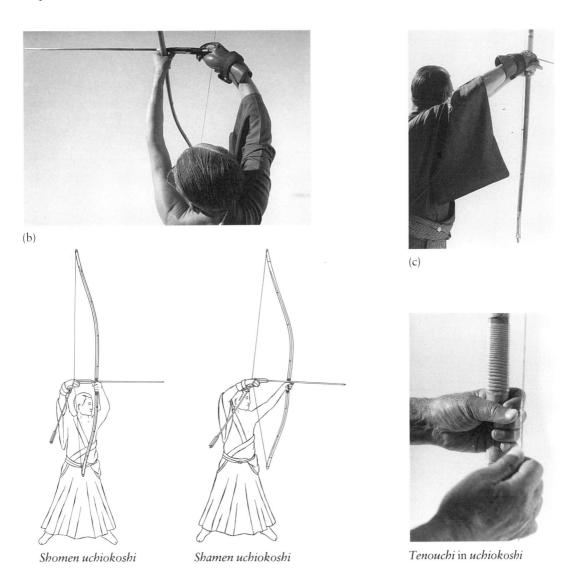

(b)

(c)

Shomen uchiokoshi   Shamen uchiokoshi   Tenouchi in uchiokoshi

Hikiwake (drawing the bow)

The Japanese bow is drawn in two steps. The first, called *daisan*, is a preliminary move that sets up the draw. *Daisan* is followed by the draw itself.

Daisan means "Big Three." The term was coined from the teaching "Push big and pull one-third." *Daisan* is formed by pushing the bow to the left as the right arm folds at the elbow. The move is complete when the arrow has been drawn about half its length and the right hand is a little above and just forward of the forehead. At this point in the draw most shooting styles pause momentarily. But even though the motion appears to stop, it is really quite active, because the pause coincides with the exhalation of the breath and the flow of the spirit.

Hikiwake (a)

The second stage of *hikiwake*, the actual drawing of the bow, begins as you start to inhale. You should continue to inhale until you have completed about one-third of the draw. You then gently settle the breath in the lower abdomen. Do not attempt to force the breath down or you will create excessive tension in the upper body musculature.

In kyudo, the bow is not so much pulled as it is spread apart. It is spread equally to the left and right, of course, but one should have the feeling that the bow is sliding along the arrow, and not the reverse. This same idea is also reflected in the teaching "Push the string with the left arm and pull the bow with the right."

The bow is drawn primarily with the back and chest muscles, and not with the arms or hands. This enables you to evenly distribute the force of the pull throughout the whole of your body, which makes for a smooth, effortless draw. During the drawing sequence from *daisan* into *kai* the left hand and the right elbow move simultaneously down and to the back along a curved path. It is almost as if the bow were trying to encompass the archer's body. To emphasize this point, master archers often tell their students to have a feeling of squeezing their body between the bow and string as they complete the draw.

(b)

Kai (completing the draw)

Kai means "Meeting." It comes from the Buddhist teaching that every meeting is followed by a separation. In kyudo this means that each of the previous stages of shooting leads to *kai*, and that the release is a natural result of their meeting. Thus, the success or failure of our shooting is not determined after the release, it is determined in *kai*.

It can be said that if *hikiwake* is the physical draw, then *kai* is the spiritual draw. In *hikiwake* the strength we use to draw the bow comes from the efficient use of our body—the working of the bones and muscles in conjunction with correct technique. But in *kai* most of the physical work has been done. It is then time for the spirit to take over, or, as some say, to "pass the baton to God."

This does not mean, however, that the physical side is totally ignored in *kai*. You must still complete what is known as the "final working" of the body—the gentle stretch of the vertical line of the neck and spine (*tatesen*), together with the horizontal line of the chest, shoulders, and arms (*yokosen*). This condition, called *tsumeai*, continues until the slack in the body has been taken up and all remaining areas of weakness have been removed. At this point the work of the body is complete since further physical effort will only create tension in the body. But you cannot stop here or *suki*, an opening or point of weakness, will be created. This is where the working of the spirit comes in. As long as it continues to flow smoothly there will be no *suki*. Assisted by the power and stability of the *tsumeai*, your spirit builds in intensity until it reaches the point where the release is inevitable. This final, all-important, working of the spirit is called *nobiai*.

For purposes of study it is necessary to separate the actions of *tsumeai* and *nobiai*. In reality, though, the two should be inseparable. We can use the following analogy to explain the relationship between

(c)

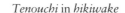

Tenouchi in *hikiwake*

tsumeai and *nobiai:* The growth of a large tree is so subtle that we cannot actually see it growing. However, if we were to watch it over a period of time we could see it blossom and bear fruit. And if we were patient enough, we could watch the fruit as it ripens, then falls, at just the right moment, from the tree. And so it is with *tsumeai* and *nobiai*. In *kai,* your body should grow subtly. It should be strong and stable, without weakness of any kind. At the same time, your spirit should expand endlessly. You must never think about when to release. You simply wait until the moment is ripe for the arrow to fly.

Kai (a)

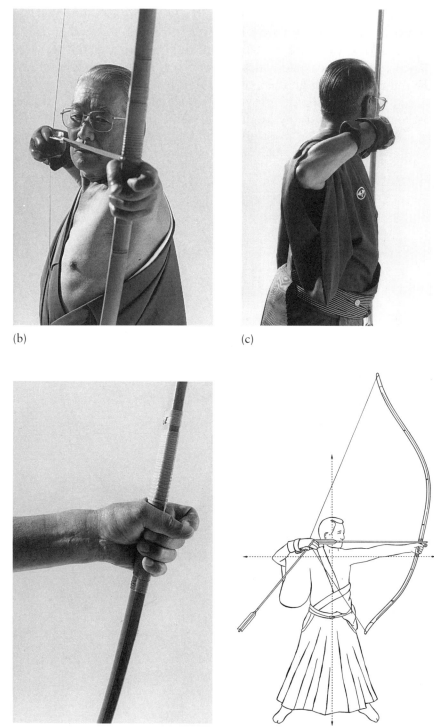

(b)

(c)

Tenouchi in *Kai*

Tatesen and *yokosen*

Breathing

The question of how to control the breath in *kai* is without a doubt one of the more difficult problems you will confront in your study of kyudo. Most master archers agree on what happens during this time, but their methods of teaching it differ considerably. This is further complicated by the fact that the same teacher might give different explanations to different students based on their level of understanding. Some instructors say to hold the breath in *kai*, while others teach their students to exhale softly. In a way both explanations are correct. If we let too much air escape while in *kai* we run the risk of destroying the *tsumeai* and *nobiai*. Thus a teacher might tell his student to hold the breath in *kai* to overcome this tendency. On the other hand, if we try to hold the breath in the upper chest we can reach a state that is painfully close to asphyxiation. In this case the teacher will tell his student to exhale.

The truth of what happens lies somewhere between these two extremes, however. As you complete *hikiwake* you must let the breath settle out of the upper chest and into the lower abdomen. To do this, you must be careful not to fill the chest cavity with too much air. Then while in *kai* you should have the feeling that the breath leaves your body as part of the *nobiai*. All of this should be nearly imperceptible. Perhaps it can best be described as exhaling through the skin.

Aiming

Although there are several methods of visually sighting the target, most teachers advise their students to aim with their spirit, or to see the target with the "eyes of the mind." The following story shows what they mean by this:

A man who wished to study the Way of the Bow traveled to a distant village to meet a great kyudo master who lived there. When he reached the master's home he asked to be accepted as a student.

"I can teach you nothing," said the master, "unless you can see properly."

"But sensei, my eyes are fine," replied the man.

"If that is so, then I assume you can see that spider climbing along the garden fence," the master replied.

"Of course," said the man, "I can see it quite clearly."

"Tell me then," asked the master, "how clear are the spots on its body?"

"Spots?" the man asked incredulously. "From this distance I cannot see any spots."

"Then come back when you can," said the master.

The man was disappointed. He was anxious to begin his study of kyudo, but he knew the master would never teach him unless he did as he was told. Reluctantly, he returned home. There, he took a small fly, tied it to a thread, and hung it in his window. Day after day he

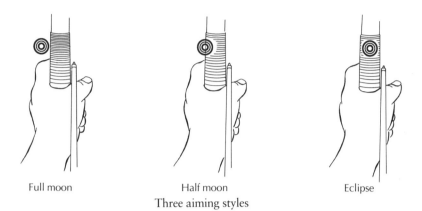

Full moon　　　　　　Half moon　　　　　　Eclipse

Three aiming styles

stared at the fly in an attempt to make it appear larger. He tried every-thing. He stared at the fly with his eyes wide open. He tried squinting, or closing one eye. At one point he even tried looking at the fly with his eyes crossed. But nothing worked. The fly always seemed like the tiny black speck that it had been when he first hung it in the window. Finally he gave up and went to the master for help.

"The secret," said the master, " is not to *look* at the object with your eyes, but to *see* it with the 'mind's eye.' "

The man did not really understand what the master meant by this, but he went home and tried to do as he was told. At first, everything was the same as before. Gradually, however, he began to see the fly in more and more detail. It actually seemed to be growing larger. Eventu-ally, he was able to make out the wings, the eyes, even the hairs on its body. It was almost as if the fly were right in front of him.

When the man was sure of his ability he went to see the master again.

"I can count the spots on the spider's body," said the man.

The master nodded his approval, then handed the man a bow and set of arrows. He pointed to a distant plum tree and told the man to shoot the lowest-hanging fruit.

"I have never shot a bow before. I'll never be able to hit the fruit," said the man.

"You have learned all that is necessary," replied the master. "Use your spirit and you will not fail."

The man drew the bow, then waited calmly for the plum to grow larger. When the plum appeared to have closed the distance and to be touching the tip of his arrow, he let the arrow fly. A moment later he watched in amazement as the arrow pierced the plum through the center. He shot again and again, each time with the same result.

Kai, more than anything else, holds the essence of kyudo. It is the point at which we are most vulnerable to our own mental and physi-cal weaknesses. For *kai* to be successful we must clear our mind of mundane thoughts, remove all attachment to the target, dispel all doubt and fear, and seek a perfect balance of mind, body, and tech-nique. Needless to say, bringing all this together at the precise moment requires a great deal of patience and practice. But it is time and effort well spent because failure to understand *kai* is a failure to understand kyudo.

Hanare (the release)

If *kai* holds the essence of kyudo, then *hanare* reveals its mystery. *Hanare* is a thing of wonder; it lies on the edge of understanding. As a result, there is no adequate way to describe it except through analogy. *Hanare* has been compared to the moment when flint and iron combine to create a spark, or to when snow falls under its own weight

Hanare

from a leaf. Both images illustrate the importance of a natural, spontaneous release. But if *hanare* is so difficult to understand, how can one learn to make a correct release? Perhaps the best method is to think of not making the release. That will usually keep the spirit flowing long enough for the release to happen naturally. Most teachers suggest waiting in *kai* for about six to eight seconds to achieve a good *hanare*. A quick release (*hayake*) does not allow enough time for the various mental and physical components of shooting to merge. And a release that comes after an extended period in *kai* (*motare*) has missed its moment of ripeness.

A true *hanare* is the product of a unified mind and body. Ushered in by the spirit, it unfolds cleanly from the center of the chest, much like a pear being split with a knife. Some teachers have their students close their eyes and hold a piece of string taut between their hands, then the teacher cuts the string in the center to teach the student the feeling of a correct *hanare*.

Watching a pure *hanare* is like witnessing the striking of a large drum. The action is over in the blink of an eye, but the power of the strike continues to be felt for some time afterward. Seeing a poor *hanare*, on the other hand, is like watching a movie of a drum being struck—but with the sound turned off.

Yugaeri

At the release, if the *tenouchi* is correct, the bow will turn in place so that the string swings around to touch the outer left arm. This action is called the *yugaeri*.

It is unclear exactly when and why the *yugaeri* was incorporated into the shooting method. Some sources suggest that it first appeared sometime around the fifteenth century when major changes were being made in both bow construction and shooting technique. It is almost certain, however, that it was first used in ceremonial archery since the warrior archer had no time in the midst of battle to return the string to its original position and set another arrow. Today, however, most shooting styles, including those based on battlefield technique, have adopted the *yugaeri*.

Anyone can make the bow turn simply by opening and closing the left hand at the moment of release to catch the bow as it turns. This is not a true *yugaeri*, however. When the *yugaeri* is correct the bow does not have to be caught by the archer. It merely spins in place after the release without dropping in the hand or tilting excessively. The technique is not easily learned. It requires a good deal of practice and a thorough understanding of *tenouchi* to truly master *yugaeri*.

Zanshin (continuation)

In kyudo, the shooting does not end with the release of the arrow, it ends with *zanshin*. *Zanshin* means "remaining body." The word is a homonym, however, so it can also mean "remaining spirit." Both definitions are used to explain the period following the release, when you continue to hold your position and send forth your spirit, even after the arrow has reached the target.

Physically, *zanshin* must be calm, dignified, and perfectly balanced. The body must be strong, but not tense; relaxed, but without any hint of weakness. Mentally, *zanshin* is a condition of supreme alertness, with the spirit flowing uninterrupted not only toward the target but in every other direction as well.

One can think of *zanshin* as being like the reverberation of a temple bell, which can be felt even past the time when the sound disappears.

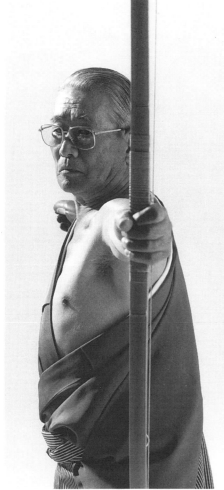

Zanshin (a)   (b)

Yudaoshi

Included within the context of *zanshin* is a separate move called *yudaoshi*, the lowering of the bow. In *yudaoshi* maintain visual contact with the target as you slowly lower your hands to your sides, so that the end of the bow is once again in line with the center of the body. Next, turn your head to face the *kamiza*. After that, step with the right foot in a half-step toward the center of the body, then bring the left foot over to meet the right, thus bringing the basic shooting procedure to a close.

Yudaoshi

CHAPTER

7

The Technique and Practice of Kyudo

There is a story in kyudo about an old master who was honored at a banquet for his outstanding archery skills. After the meal the participants retired to another room for tea. There, in one corner, stood a beautiful bow and set of arrows. The master complimented his host on their grace and beauty, then innocently asked what they were used for.

This story is not unique to kyudo. In one form or another it is used in the martial arts to convey the idea that the master, having gone full circle, returns to the pure innocence of the beginner. But, like the hands of a clock that start and finish at twelve, there is one important difference between the master and the beginner: Time.

Time equals experience, both technical and practical. There may be someone out there who can unlock the secrets of kyudo through spirit alone, but for most of us it also takes technical proficiency and constant practice.

Kyudo Technique

They say that technique is the stairway to the spiritual level. Before you can know what true kyudo is, you must first have the experience of knowing that every time you shoot you will not miss the target. This in itself is not kyudo, but it is a necessary step.

The study of technique, then, is an important part of the learning experience. But overdependence on technique is self-limiting. The solution, as always, is to balance your training. There is a time to study technique, and a time to forget it. When you learn something new you must practice it until it "melts into your blood" and becomes a natural part of you. Then you must let it go.

Learning kyudo technique is like learning anything else. We start with the basics, then gradually advance to the higher levels, much like a child learns to write the alphabet. There is no way, for example, for the child to skip the first stages of writing. She learns by imitation, but if she tries to imitate beyond her level of comprehension—as when she tries to mimic the handwriting of an adult—she will only succeed in making an unintelligible mess. Even so, from time to time she should be encouraged to watch and follow the writing style of an adult. That, after all, instills in the child the desire to learn and encourages her to progress from one stage to the next.

Basic Technique and Instruction

Obviously there is more than one way to teach kyudo. Given kyudo's history and development it is only natural for there to be a variety of techniques and teaching methods. The techniques and instructions included here were chosen to make your study of kyudo easier. Even so, they can never be a substitute for the knowledge and guidance of a qualified teacher.

No teacher, however, not even a great one, can teach kyudo if the student does not have a sincere desire to learn. The most basic of all techniques, then, is learning how to learn. And the best way to learn kyudo is to practice, while keeping the following points in mind:
• Be flexible and openminded. Resist the temptation to reject any teaching that doesn't seem to fit your particular ideas at the time.
• Learn to practice on your own. The instructor can show you the way, but you must make the journey.
• Be attentive. Do not expect to be actively taught all the time. "Steal" from the teacher by watching and copying his actions and manner.
• Always do your best. Never accept mediocrity in yourself. Above all, strive for correctness in mind, body, and technique.
• Be well-mannered and humble. Ask questions, but never question the answers. And never make excuses when corrected by the teacher.
• Periodically return to the basics. When you are lost or confused, they are the ideal place to make a fresh start.

In addition, the Zen Nihon Kyudo Renmei lists these five elements as fundamental to all shooting:

1. Bow Strength/Body Strength

In order to achieve a natural draw, the pull strength of the bow must correspond to the strength of the archer.

2. Basic Form

The so-called three- and five-cross relationships; the vertical and horizontal alignment of the body, bow, arrow, and glove.

3. Breath Control

Breathing in kyudo is not just the physiological process of inhaling and exhaling. It is the conscious ordering of the breath so that it blends smoothly with the movement of the body and the flow of the spirit.

4. Eye Control

The movement and direction of the eyes must be carefully controlled throughout the shooting procedure.

5. The Working of the Spirit

A strong spirit is the product of strict self-control and emotional stability.

The following techniques and teaching points are meant to supplement your study of the *hassetsu*, the eight basic stages of shooting. Therefore, if you are new to kyudo you should first have a good working knowledge of the *hassetsu* (see Chapter 6) before starting this section.

Three-cross Relationship

The alignment of the spine with the:
(1) Shoulders
(2) Hips
(3) Feet

Five-cross Relationship

The alignment of the:
(1) Bow and arrow
(2) Bow and *tenouchi*
(3) Neck and arrow
(4) Right thumb and string
(5) Shoulders and center line
    of the chest

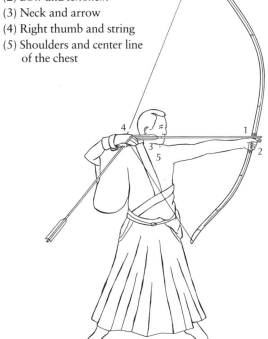

Ashibumi

To make a smooth *ashibumi*, never shift your body or bend your legs when stepping. It is often helpful to think of spreading your feet as you would unfold a fan.

If *ashibumi* is wider than normal, the body will be stable from the sides but far too weak from the front and back. Also, the arrow may fly high. Conversely, if the footing is too narrow, the body will be stable from the front and back but will have a tendency to lean to the left or right. Also, the arrow may fly too low.

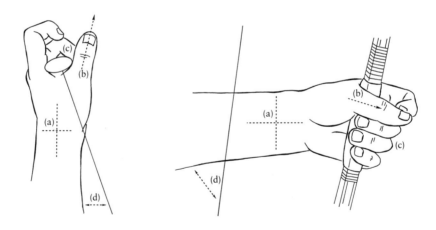

Keep these four points in mind when making *tenouchi*:

(a) Keep the wrist perfectly straight.
(b) Have the feeling of pushing the thumb forward along the top of the middle finger.
(c) Keep the bow pressed against the hand by working the last three fingers as if they were one.
(d) Hold the bow so that when the string is not under tension it is about five centimeters away from the forearm.

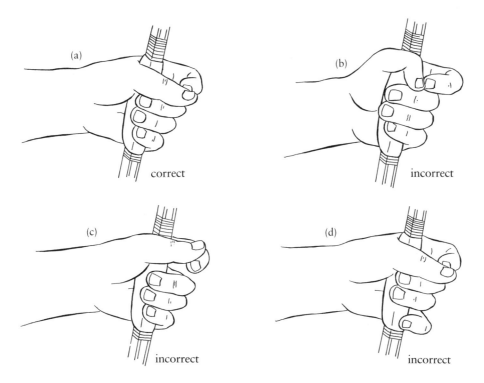

(a) correct
(b) incorrect
(c) incorrect
(d) incorrect

Tenouchi

If the *tenouchi* is correct the hand will appear slim and streamlined with a small space between the base of the thumb and the grip (a). Do not make a fist or hold the bow as you would hold a stick (b). And never lose the connection between the thumb and fingers (c) or between the little finger and the bow (d).

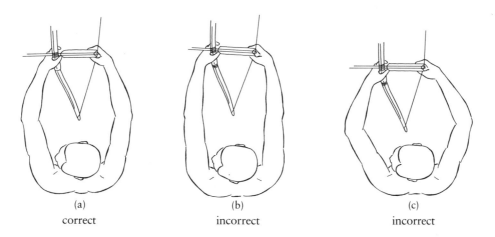

(a) correct
(b) incorrect
(c) incorrect

Uchiokoshi

Keep the arms naturally rounded when raising the bow (a). They should be neither too straight (b) nor too round (c).

Daisan

To make *daisan*, fold and lift the right elbow while pushing the left arm outward and upward. The saying, "Hang the earth from your right elbow and push your left hand to the sky" is used to teach this point.

Hikiwake

To draw the *yumi* do not use a horizontal push and pull of the left and right arms as you would in Western archery (a). Think, instead, of arcing back the right elbow so that it sets behind the shoulder in *kai* (b). At the same time, push from the left shoulder as you guide the front arm down and to the left (c).

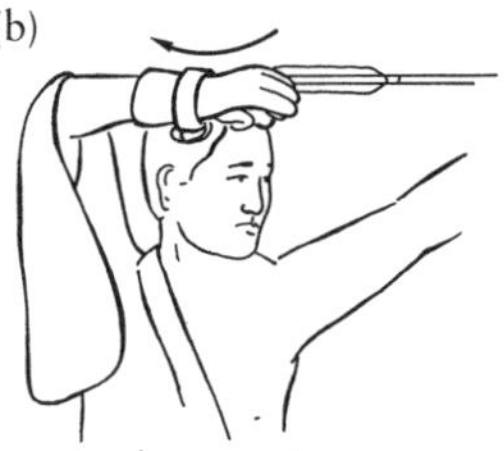

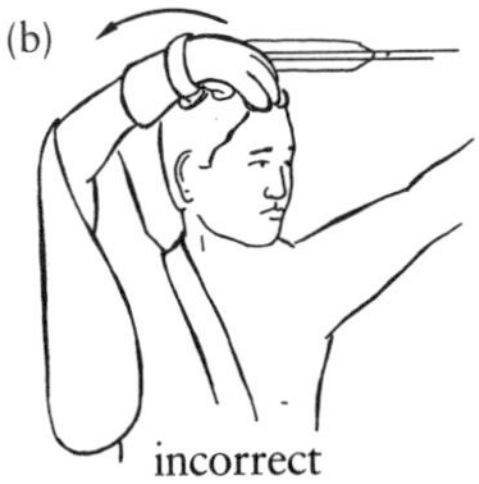

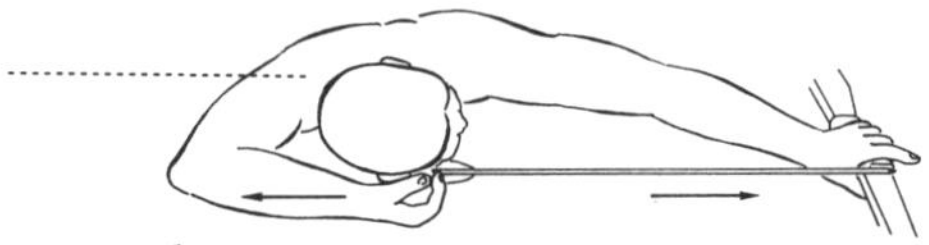

(a)

(b) correct

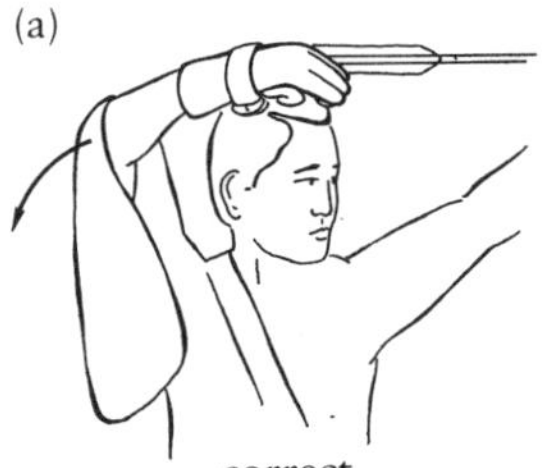

(b) incorrect

(b) incorrect

(a)
Western archery

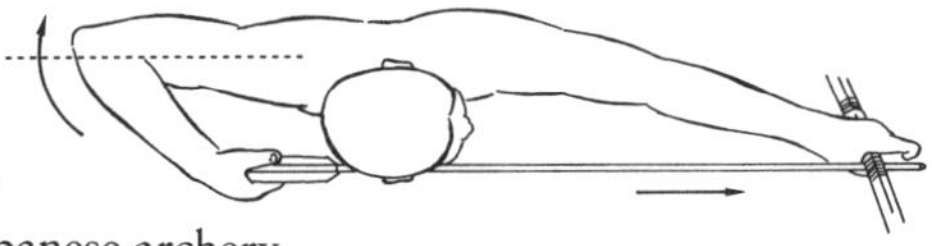

(b)
Japanese archery

(c)

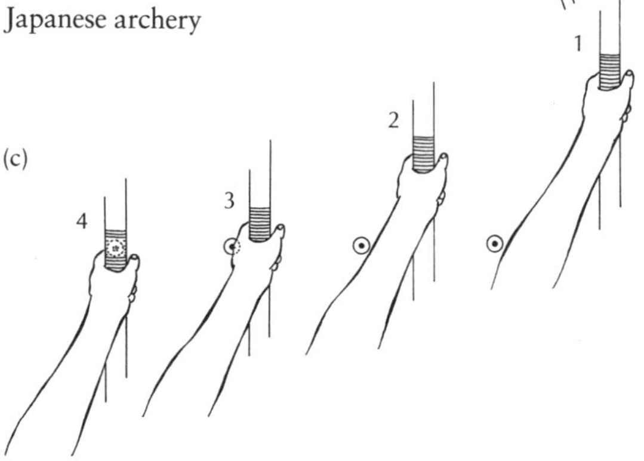

(c)

(d) 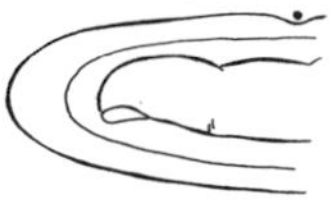 correct

(e) incorrect

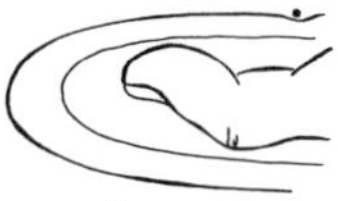

Always think of pulling the bow with the elbow (a), not with the hand (b). You should have the feeling that the string pulls the glove (c). Always keep your thumb straight inside the glove (d). Do not try to "hold" the string with your own thumb (e).

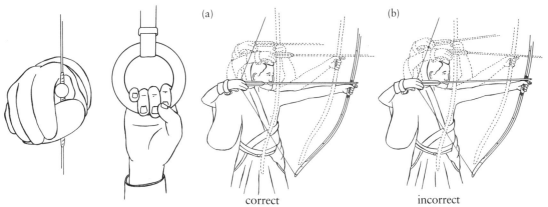

(a)   (b)

correct   incorrect

Torikake

The fingers of the right hand hold the thumb much as you would hold the safety ring on a train or bus.

Hikiwake

Throughout the process of drawing the bow, the arrow must be kept horizontal (a). Do not pull in stages or rock between the left and right sides (b).

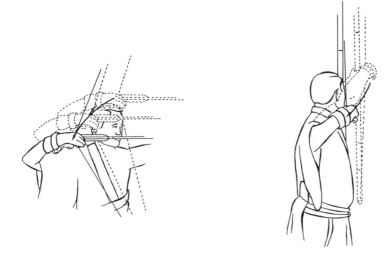

The path of the string from *daisan* into *kai*.

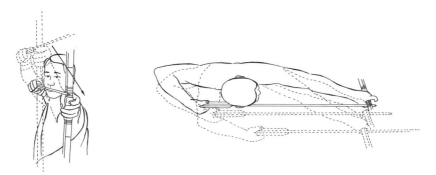

The path of the arrow from *daisan* into *kai*.

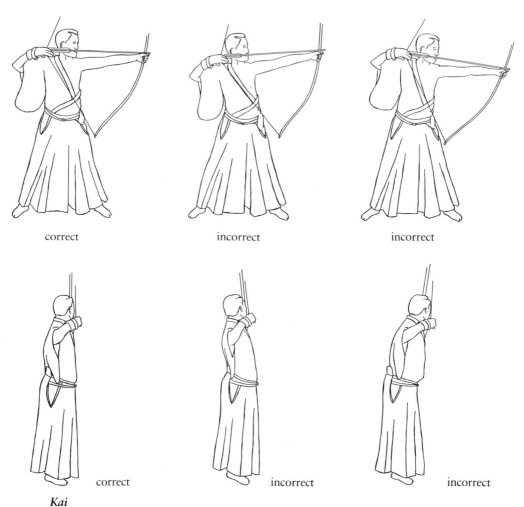

correct   incorrect   incorrect

correct   incorrect   incorrect

Kai

Stand straight in *kai*. Be careful not to lean excessively to the front, back, left, or right.

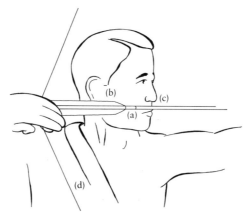

In *kai* the arrow is drawn so that the *motohagi*, the bottom feather binding, is positioned a couple of centimeters behind the corner of the mouth (a). The arrow is pressed lightly against the side of the face (b), with the shaft placed between the mouth and nose (c). The string should lightly touch the chest (d).

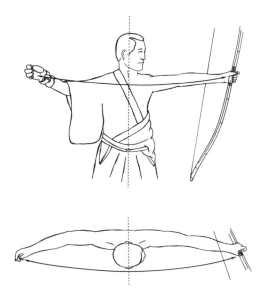

Hanare

At the release think of unfolding evenly from the center of the chest.

Intermediate Technique and Instruction

Once you have a thorough understanding of the basics it is time to further refine your technique. The teachings presented here should complement the teachings you learned in the previous section. Try not to think of them as separate or unrelated.

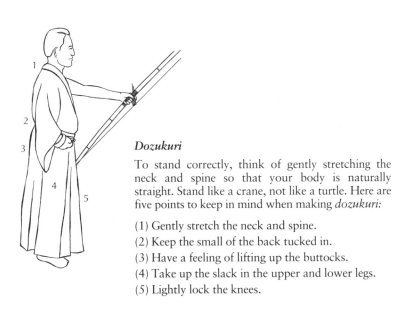

Dozukuri

To stand correctly, think of gently stretching the neck and spine so that your body is naturally straight. Stand like a crane, not like a turtle. Here are five points to keep in mind when making *dozukuri:*

(1) Gently stretch the neck and spine.
(2) Keep the small of the back tucked in.
(3) Have a feeling of lifting up the buttocks.
(4) Take up the slack in the upper and lower legs.
(5) Lightly lock the knees.

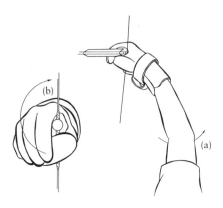

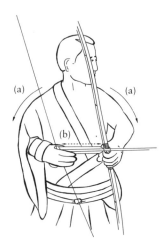

Torikake

To make *torikake*, think of rotating your whole arm. Do this with a feeling of pushing from under the elbow (a). This movement will transfer to the hand so that the thumb pushes up and outward, and the forefinger rotates to hold the arrow in place (b).

Habiki

After completing the *tenouchi* and *torikake*, gently spread your back and shoulders to take up the slack in your arms (a). This action, called the *habiki*, will cause the string to be pulled slightly so that the feathers can clear the bow (b).

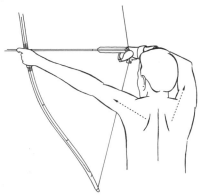

Daisan

As you move into *daisan* take up the slack by stretching from the shoulder blades.

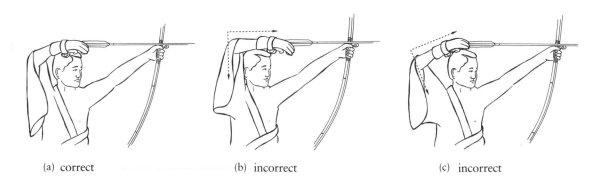

(a) correct   (b) incorrect   (c) incorrect

In *daisan* keep the right arm relaxed and natural looking (a). Do not hold the arm so that it appears stiff or angular (b and c).

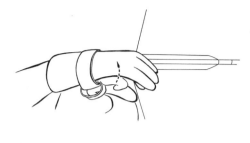

Hikiwake

In *hikiwake* you should have the feeling that the front arm is leading the draw. Push the left shoulder forward and pull from the back of the upper right arm.

In *hikiwake* and *kai* have the feeling of lifting the little finger of the right hand up and outward.

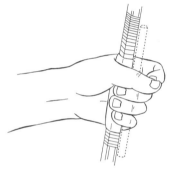

Kai

In *kai* have the feeling of pushing your right shoulder toward the strap of the glove.

Tenouchi

In *kai* hold the bow so that a little space—enough to insert an arrow—remains between the grip and the last three fingers.

In *kai* equally stretch the vertical and horizontal lines of the body. The vertical line makes the body strong from the front and back, and the horizontal line makes the body strong from the sides.

Hanare

Sometimes the arms will drop or jump at the release. To correct this, imagine that you are pushing your left thumb into the center of the target, and that you are striking a big drum with the back of your right hand.

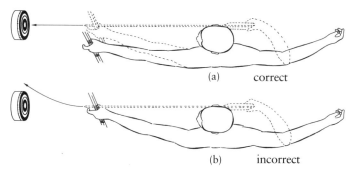

At the release, open from the center of the chest. This moves the front arm a little to the left so that the arrow flies straight (a). Do not hold the left arm rigidly in place or the bow will impede the flight of the arrow (b).

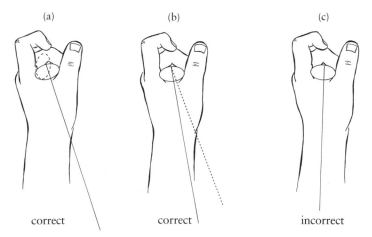

Yugaeri

The *yugaeri*, the turning of the bow, is the product of a correct *tenouchi*. From *uchiokoshi* into *daisan* let the bow turn so that it is held at a slight angle (a). Then, from *daisan* into *kai* increase the pressure of the grip and the push of the thumb so that, in *kai*, the bow is held nearly square in the hand but remains under light tension. The bow should return to its previous position if the string is not being pulled (b). This is the working force behind the *yugaeri*. Do not let the bow turn completely in *daisan* (c). This will cause the string to hit the forearm upon release.

Advanced Technique and Instruction

Because of its subtlety, advanced technique cannot be completely and clearly presented in written form. Therefore, you may need to rely on the help and guidance of a qualified instructor to fully understand the teachings in this section.

(a) (b)

correct   incorrect

Uchiokoshi

From *uchiokoshi* into *daisan* have the feeling of pushing the underside of both arms outward while keeping the chest "hollow" (a). Do not pinch the shoulders against the neck (b).

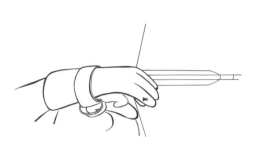

Hikiwake

When you draw the bow keep your hand relaxed so that you can feel the thumb of the glove press against the first joint of the last finger on the glove.

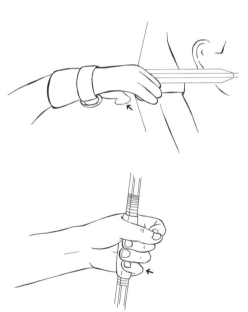

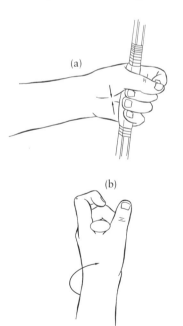

(a)

(b)

Tenouchi

In *hikiwake* and *kai* apply even pressure to both little fingers.

In *tenouchi* think of pressing the root of the thumb and the base of the little finger together (a). Also have a slight feeling of twisting the hand to the right (b).

Kai

Kyudo is not only a matter of pushing and pulling with your arms. You must shoot with your whole body. Think of making an "X" with your body: from the right heel through the abdomen into the left arm, and from the left toes through the abdomen into the right elbow.

Do not rely on the power of the muscles alone. Correct alignment of the skeletal structure is a crucial element of shooting. Stretch to a "protective position," as if you were trying to keep a wall from closing in on you. Overstretching or failure to stretch adequately will cause the muscles to work excessively, resulting in a poor release.

(a) correct

(b) incorrect

(c) incorrect

(d) incorrect

In *kai* keep the shoulder blades flat while you make the muscles between them firm. Use the muscles of the lower back and stretch upward and outward through the shoulder blades (a). Do not squeeze the shoulder blades together (b) or lose the symmetry between them (c and d).

In *kai* check the following points:

> Stretch the horizontal line of the body (*yokosen*).
> Stretch the vertical line of the body (*tatesen*).
> Press both shoulders toward the arrow shaft.
> Keep both elbows parallel to the floor.
> Keep the left wrist straight.
> Push the left thumb forward.
> Keep the right wrist straight.
> Set the right elbow behind the right shoulder.
> Keep the head straight and faced toward the target.
> Press the arrow lightly against the cheek.
> Touch the string against the chest.
> Stretch the inner thighs.
> Lightly lock the knees.
> Center the weight of the body between both feet.
> Keep the chest relaxed.
> Settle the breath in the lower abdomen.
> Keep the eyes soft.
> Keep the spirit flowing in all directions.

Nerai

When taking aim do not look down the arrow. Look at the target with the left eye as you sight through the bow with the right eye.

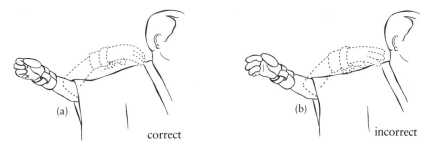

(a) correct   (b) incorrect

Hanare

At the release let the fingers slip off the thumb naturally (a). Do not open the fingers to make the release (b).

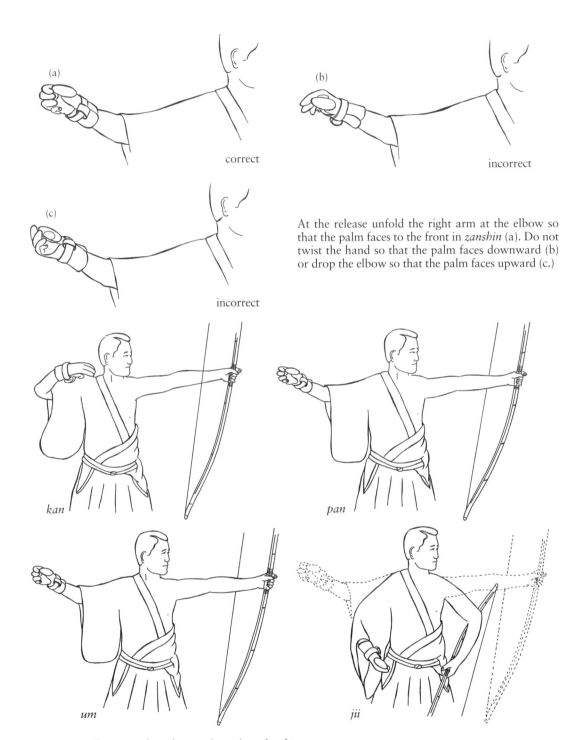

(a)

correct

(b)

incorrect

(c)

incorrect

At the release unfold the right arm at the elbow so that the palm faces to the front in *zanshin* (a). Do not twist the hand so that the palm faces downward (b) or drop the elbow so that the palm faces upward (c.)

kan

pan

um

jii

The timing from *hanare* through *yudaoshi*

To learn the timing from *hanare* through *yudaoshi* think of these four sounds: *Kan, Pan, Um, Jii. Kan* refers to the sound of the string upon the release, *Pan* is the sound of the arrow penetrating the target, *Um* represents the feeling of sending forth the spirit in *zanshin*, and *Jii* approximates the time it takes to lower the arms in *yudaoshi*.

Breathing

Proper control of the breath is undoubtedly the most important technique you can learn in kyudo. It is also the most difficult. Generally speaking, breath follows movement: Breathe in at the start of the movement and out at its finish. As a rule, large movements require longer breaths while small movements either use shorter breaths or combine to blend with the rhythm of a longer breath. In all cases the breathing must be smooth, rhythmical, and natural. Never allow the breathing to become forced or mechanical.

 (1) Inhale as you begin *ashibumi*.
 (2) Exhale as you finish *ashibumi*.
 (3) Inhale as you begin *dozukuri*.
 (4) Exhale as you finish *dozukuri*.
 (5) Inhale as you begin *yugamae*.
 (6) Exhale as you finish *yugamae*.
 (7) Inhale as you begin *uchiokoshi*.
 (8) Exhale as you finish *uchiokoshi*.
 (9) Inhale as you move into *daisan*.
(10) Exhale as you finish *daisan*.
(11) Inhale until you have drawn to about midface in *hikiwake*.
(12) As you complete *hikiwake* gently settle the breath in the lower abdomen. Do not attempt to force the breath down.
(13) In *kai* you should have the feeling that the breath leaves your body as part of the *nobiai*. All of this should be nearly imperceptible, as if exhaling through the skin.
(14) At *hanare* release "one bean's worth" of air with the *kiai*.
(15) In *zanshin* continue with the feeling that the breath is leaving your body through the skin.
(16) Exhale as you make *yudaoshi*.

1   2   3   4

5   6   7

8   9   10

11

12

13

14

15

16

Standard Practice Methods

It is said that shooting begins and ends with courtesy. But it was not always so. In the Heian period, ceremonial shooting and shooting technique were separate. The ceremony belonged to the court nobles and Shinto priests, and technique belonged to the samurai. Eventually, however, both sides realized that etiquette and technique were equally important. The ceremonial archers found that without adequate technique the ceremony was incomplete. And the samurai realized that the ceremony was an excellent way to train the spirit. It made it possible for them to combine their study of the bow with the study of themselves, a definite plus for men whose lives depended not only on the strength of their technique but also on the strength of their character.

Today, advanced ceremonial shooting is performed by archers of great skill and experience. Consequently, it lies outside the sphere of practice of most *kyudojo*, where daily training tends to center around simple *makiwara* or target practice. The standard practice methods presented here, both seated and standing, are semiformal shooting procedures. These are used not only for daily practice but for contests and examinations as well. Therefore, when practicing these procedures you should try to exhibit a high degree of grace and refinement, just as the masters do when they perform a formal shooting ceremony.

When you visit a Japanese *kyudojo*, you will hear the instructor refer often to a student's *taihai*. *Taihai* means "form" and correct form is a product of correct posture and correct movement.

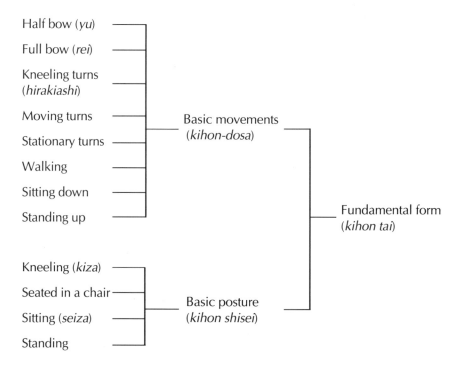

Kyudo form is divided into four basic postures: standing; sitting in a chair while waiting for one's turn to shoot; *kiza*, a special way of kneeling; and *seiza*, a formal method of sitting on the floor. In all cases the head, neck, and spine are kept straight, the chest and shoulders are kept naturally relaxed, and the weight of the body is centered in the lower abdomen. The eyes look forward along the line of the nose to a point on the floor four meters away when standing, three meters away when sitting, and two meters away when kneeling in *kiza* or *seiza*. It is also important to keep the mouth closed at all times and to hold the fingers together in a relaxed manner. As a general rule, men stand with their feet about three centimeters apart, and women keep their feet together. Women also keep their knees together when in *seiza* or *kiza*, but men sit with their knees spread about one fist's width apart.

Contrary to what some people think, kyudo is not practiced in slow motion. The movement is controlled, yes, but it is controlled by the breath. We do not breathe in slow motion, we breathe with a natural, harmonious rhythm. In kyudo, every movement—walking, turning, standing, sitting, and bowing—follows the rhythm of the breath, bringing vitality and a quiet strength to the shooting.

(a)   *Kiza*   (b)   *Kiza*

(a)   *Seiza*   (b)   *Seiza*

One way to develop such movement is to think of using your entire body to move just one finger. Another way is to think of sending your spirit ahead of every move you make. When walking, think not of moving the legs but of pushing the center of the body forward, as if walking against a strong wind, but with the body held straight. Turns are made by keeping the face in line with the center of the chest and synchronizing the movement of the upper body, hips, legs, and feet. The footwork will vary according to the ceremony, but, in general, turns are done at right angles. To sit or stand, think of carefully sinking or floating into position without shifting from side to side. When bowing, keep the back and neck straight and bend forward from the waist. In a full bow (*rei*) the standard angle of the bend is about forty-five degrees. To make a halfbow (*yu*), bend the upper body forward about ten centimeters to an angle of twenty degrees.

When training, it is all too easy to get caught up in the practice of shooting technique and ignore one's *taihai*. But to disregard *taihai* is to rob kyudo of much of its beauty, grace, and dignity. It is crucial, then, to practice the shooting methods often, paying close attention to *taihai*, and resist the temptation to just shoot arrows at the target.

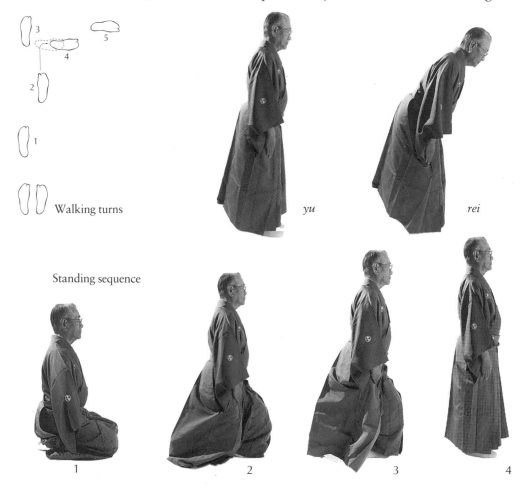

Walking turns

yu

rei

Standing sequence

1   2   3   4

Seated Practice

Most *kyudojo* use the seated form for daily practice. Shooting is usually done in rotation, with small groups of four or five archers shooting two arrows in turn. The preliminary moves—walking, kneeling, and readying the bow and arrows—are done in unison, with the first archer taking the lead. Once the preliminary moves have been completed the first archer stands and begins the *hassetsu*. In daily practice the other archers normally do not begin the *hassetsu* sequence until the archer directly in front of them has completed *dozukuri*. Also, as a basic courtesy, an archer will not begin *uchiokoshi* until the archer in front of him has completed *hanare*.

1

2

3

4

5

1   At the starting line (*honza*) kneel in *kiza,* facing the target. Rest the end of the bow on the floor directly in front of you.

2   Make a halfbow (*yu*) to the target.

3-4   Raise your body to a half-kneeling position. Set your left foot beside your right knee and stand up, keeping the end of the bow raised about ten centimeters above the floor. As you complete the movement slide your right foot forward to meet the left.

5-6   Beginning with the left foot and ending with the right, walk forward to the shooting line (*shai*).
In most kyudojo *the distance is three steps.*

7-8   Step your right foot back a half step and sink into *kiza.* Slide your right knee forward to meet the left as you complete the movement.

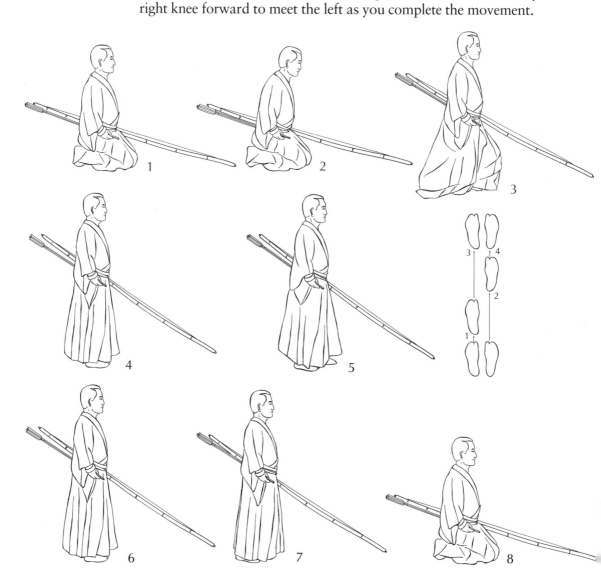

9-10 Raise your body to a half-kneeling position. At the same time raise the end of the bow to eye level. Moving from the center of the body, make *hirikiashi* (a kneeling turn) and face the *kamiza* (upper seat).

11-13 Set the bow vertically in front of you. Grasp the string from the outside with your right hand and turn the bow.

14-17 Hold both arrows parallel to the floor and look at the feathers to find the first arrow (*haya*). Extend your right hand past your left and take hold of the *haya* with your left thumb and forefinger. Move your right hand back along the arrow shaft and take hold of the nock. Slide the *haya* through the fingers of your left hand until the nock is a centimeter or so from the string. Nock the arrow so that the running feather (*hashiriba*) is on top.

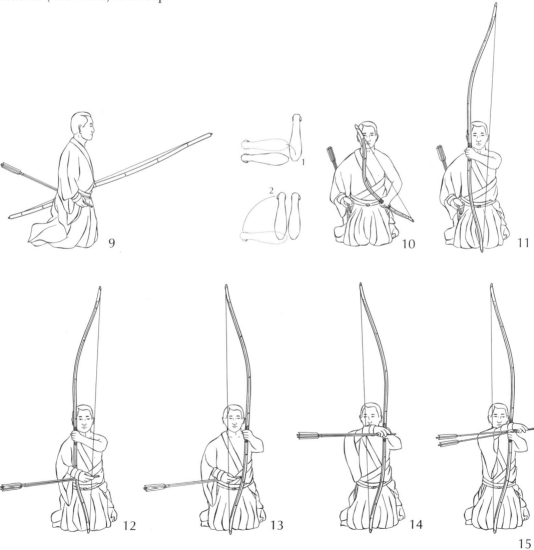

18-19 Hold the second arrow (*otoya*) vertically, then place it between the fingers of your left hand so that the arrow extends about ten centimeters beyond the string. *When shooting in a group, you must set your second arrow in unison with those in front of you. If you complete the nocking of your first arrow before the others, wait with the second arrow held vertically until they are ready.*

20 Place your right hand on your hip with the elbow pointing outward.
If you are shooting in a group, wait your turn in this position.

21-22 Raise your body to a half-kneeling position. Set your left foot beside your right knee and stand up. Slide your right foot forward to meet the left as you complete the movement.

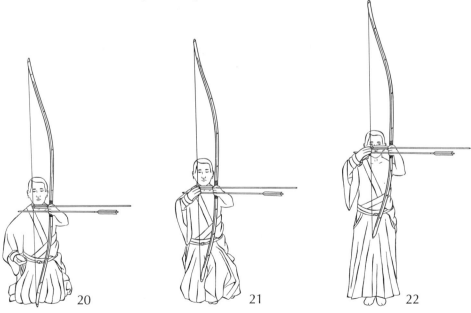

23-25 Look at the target and position the feet in *ashibumi*.

26-29 Turn your head to once again face the *kamiza*. Rest the end of the bow on your left knee then place your right hand on your hip and make *dozukuri*. Grasp the *otoya* in your right hand and place your hand on your hip. As you do so, once again check the posture of your upper body.

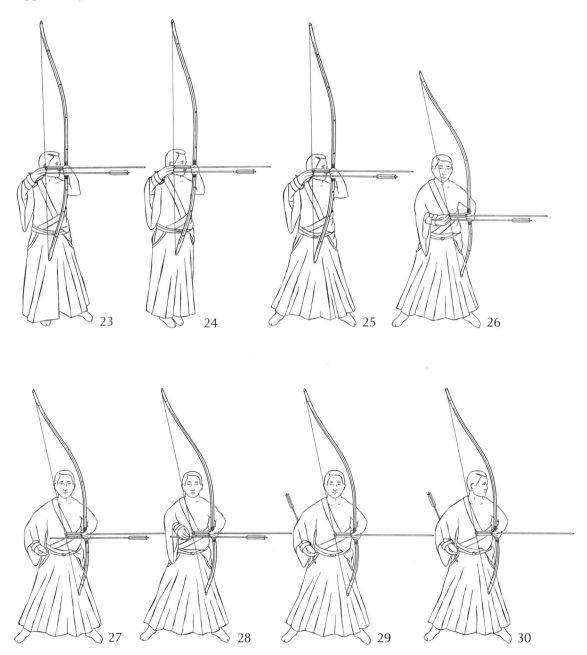

30-32 Inspect the string (*tsurushirabe*) and look down the length of the arrow toward the target. After a brief moment, look back again to the nocking area. Set the glove (*torikake*), prepare the *tenouchi*, and do *monomi* to complete *yugamae*.

33 Do *uchiokoshi* by lifting the bow straight up in front of you until you reach a point where the hands are just above the head.

34-35 Begin *hikiwake* by drawing the bow to about half the arrow's length (*daisan*). After a slight pause, continue until you have completed the draw (*kai*).

36　After the release (*hanare*), momentarily hold your body position as you send your spirit to the target in *zanshin*.

37-38　To complete *yudaoshi*, bring both hands to your sides, then turn your head to face the *kamiza*.

39-40　Close *ashibumi* by first sliding your right foot in to the center line of your body, then move the left foot over to meet the right.

36

37

38

39

40

To shoot the *otoya*, kneel once more and repeat steps 11-40. When finished, slide the right foot a half step forward and to the right to move away from the *shai*. Then, beginning with the left foot, leave the shooting area.

Standing Practice

If one has difficulty kneeling, the shooting procedure may be carried out entirely from the standing position.

1   At the *honza* stand facing the target. Keep the end of the bow raised about ten centimeters above the floor.

2   Make a halfbow (*yu*) to the target.

3-6   Beginning with the left foot, advance to the *shai* and proceed directly into *ashibumi.*

7-9   Turn your head to face the *kamiza*. Relax your grip on the bow and let it turn in your hand, then raise the bow vertically in front of you.

10-13   Hold both arrows parallel to the floor and look at the feathers to find the *haya*. Extend your right hand past your left and take hold of the *haya* with your left thumb and forefinger. Move your right hand back along the arrow shaft and take hold of the nock. Slide the *haya* through the fingers of your left hand until the nock is a centimeter or so from the string. Nock the arrow so that the *hashiriba* is on top.

14-19   Hold the *otoya* vertically, then place it between the fingers of your left hand so that the arrow extends about ten centimeters beyond the string. *When shooting in a group, you must set your second arrow in unison with those in front of you. If you complete the nocking of your first arrow before the others, wait with the second arrow held vertically until they are ready.* Rest the end of the bow on your left knee then place your right hand on your hip and make *dozukuri*. Grasp the *otoya* in your right hand and place your hand on your hip. As you do so, once again check the posture of your upper body.

7   8   9   10   11

12   13   14   15

16   17   18   19

20-28 From *yugamae* through *yudaoshi* follow the shooting procedure outlined in steps 30-38 of the seated form.

To shoot the *otoya*, repeat steps 8-28. When finished, close *ashibumi* and leave the shooting area as you would in the seated form.

20

21

22

23

24

25

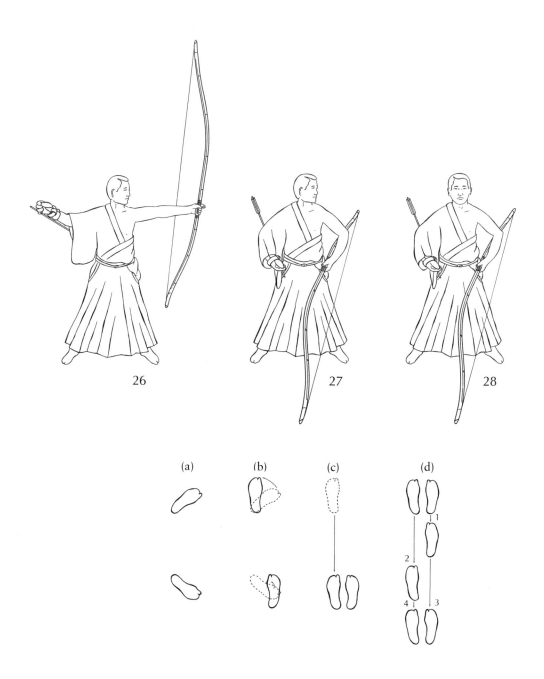

26   27   28

(a)   (b)   (c)   (d)

Note: *When shooting together with archers who are doing the seated form, wait at the* shai *until they are seated. Then, as they turn to face the* kamiza, *take a halfstep forward with your right foot and position the feet in* ashibumi. *Also, unless you are shooting last in the group, you must return to the* honza *after shooting your first arrow so that you do not disturb the seated archers. To do this, remain in* ashibumi *and turn in place to face the target. Next, slide your left foot back to meet the right. Then, beginning with the right foot, walk backward to the* honza *and wait until the last person has shot before returning to the* shai.

Dealing With Errors (*Shitsu*)

In the course of shooting you may accidentally drop the bow or an arrow, or break a string. Errors of this kind are called *shitsu* in kyudo, and specific methods of dealing with *shitsu* have been developed to minimize their effect on the beauty and harmony of the shooting procedure.

Procedure for retrieving a dropped bow

1-2   Complete *zanshin* and make *yudaoshi*. Close *ashibumi* by stepping in the direction of the bow.

3-7   Kneel in *kiza* and slide next to the bow. *If the bow is too distant, first walk to it and then kneel down.* If the string is facing you use the left hand to pick it up and turn the bow over. Take hold of the grip and bring the bow to your side.

8-11   Remain in *kiza* and slide over to your shooting place. *If the distance is great, stand and, beginning with the right foot, walk backward to your shooting place and kneel in* kiza. Bow slightly to express your apologies, then wait until it is time to prepare the *otoya* for shooting.

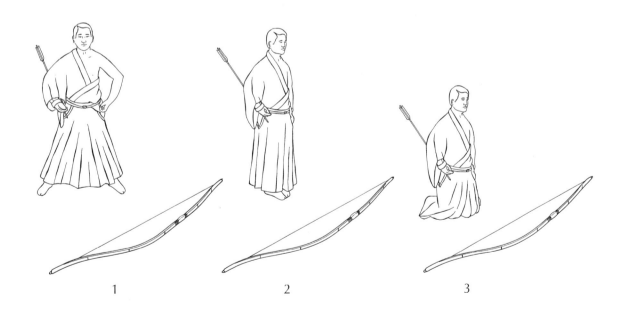

1   2   3

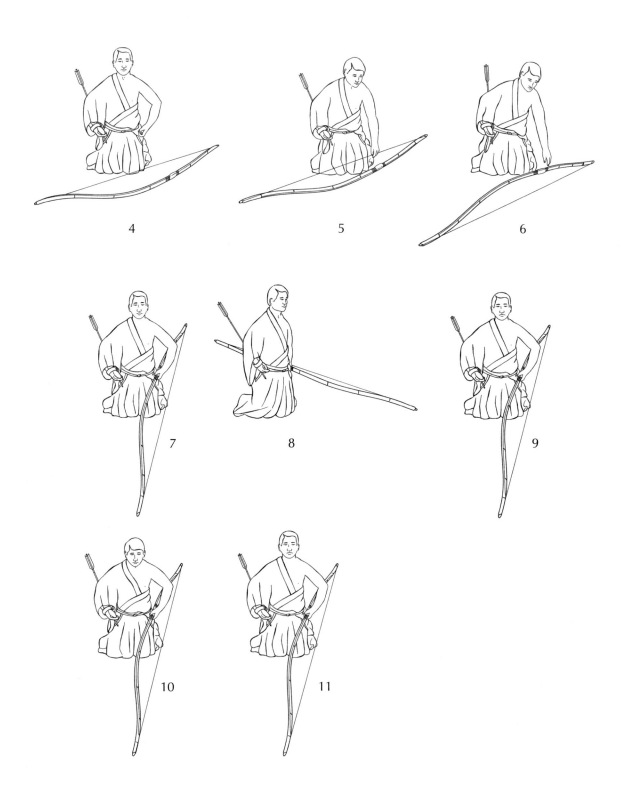

Procedure for retrieving a dropped arrow

1-2   Complete *zanshin* and make *yudaoshi*. Close *ashibumi* by stepping in the direction of the dropped arrow.

3-5   Kneel in *kiza* and slide over to the arrow. *If the arrow is too distant, first walk to it and then kneel down.* Next, transfer the *otoya* to your left hand.

6-10 Grasp the nock of the dropped arrow with your right hand and draw it alongside your right leg. Pick up the arrow and move it to your left side, underneath the *otoya*. Grasp both arrows with your right hand and bring them to your right side.

11-16 Remain in *kiza* and slide over to your shooting place. *If the distance is great, stand and, beginning with the right foot, walk backward to your shooting place and kneel in* kiza. Lay the dropped arrow on the floor in front of you so that it can be retrieved by another member of the *kyudojo*. Bow slightly to express your apologies, then wait until it is time to prepare the *otoya* for shooting. *If no one is available to assist you, lay the dropped arrow on the floor in front of you, then prepare and shoot the second arrow. When you have finished, pick up the dropped arrow and leave the shooting area.*

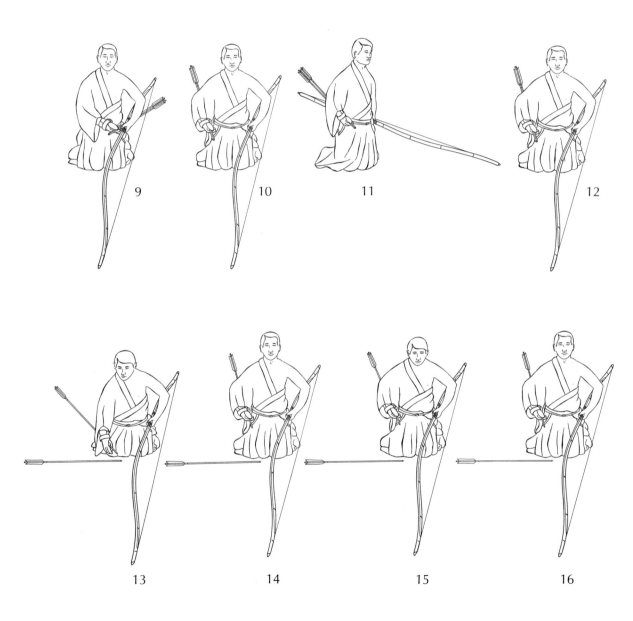

9

10

11

12

13

14

15

16

Procedure for retrieving a broken string

1-2   Complete *zanshin* and make *yudaoshi*. Close *ashibumi* by stepping in the direction of the string.

3-5   Kneel in *kiza* and slide over to the string. *If the string is too distant, first walk to it and then kneel down.* Next, transfer the *otoya* to your left hand.

6-7   With your right hand, pick up the end of the string closest to you and bring it to your left hand. Hold the end with your left thumb and forefinger as you wind the string around the other fingers.

8-9   When you have finished, grasp the *otoya* with your right hand and bring it to your right side, leaving the string in your left hand.

10-13 Remain in *kiza* and slide over to your shooting place. *If the distance is great, stand and, beginning with the right foot, walk backward to your shooting place and kneel in* kiza. Bow slightly to express your apologies and wait for another member of the *kyudojo* to come and retrieve the bow.

14-18 When the person assisting you arrives, simultaneously hand over the bow and string. Wait with your hands at your sides until your bow is restrung and returned to you. Bow slightly to the person assisting you to express your gratitude, then wait until it is time to prepare the *otoya* for shooting. *If no one is available to assist you, stand, turn in place, and walk backward to the* honza. *Leave the shooting area, replace the string, then return to your shooting place to shoot the second arrow.*

1   2   3

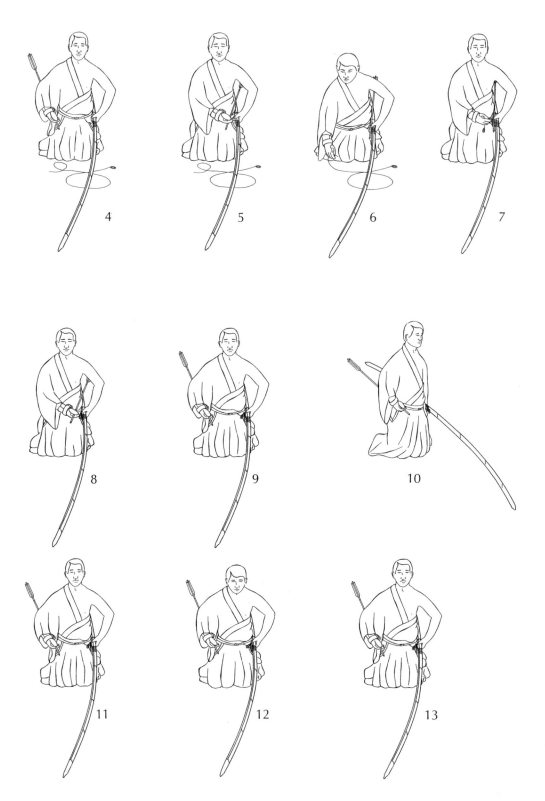

4

5

6

7

8

9

10

11

12

13

14   15   16

17   18

Notes: *If a* shitsu *occurs on the second shot, return to your shooting place after retrieving the dropped item, bow to express your apologies, then stand and leave the shooting area as you would in a normal shooting situation.*
While an archer is dealing with a shitsu, *the archer that follows must cease all activity and return to the* dozukuri *position.*

C H A P T E R
8

Problem-Solving

No one can predict the kinds of problems you will have when shooting—there are just too many mental and physical variables. Nevertheless, most of the problems you will face in kyudo will not be unique to you. Almost everyone experiences similar problems at similar stages of his or her development.

Of course, many of them will be difficult to solve, or even recognize, on your own—you will need to rely on the help of a qualified instructor. Even so, awareness of some of the more common problems and some possible solutions can greatly improve your ability to comprehend the teachings of your instructor.

PROBLEM	PROBABLE CAUSES	SOLUTION

 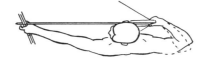 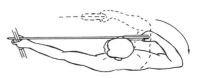

The arrow hits left of center.

The right elbow is forward in *kai*.

From *daisan* draw the elbow in an arcing motion so that it sets behind the right shoulder in *kai*.

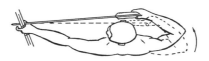 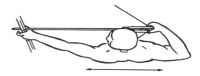

The right arm gives in at the release.

Stretch to the left and right from the center of the back.

The left wrist is bent to the left.

Keep the wrist straight by aligning the bones of the wrist and arm. Do not rely on the wrist muscles to hold the bow in place.

The left foot is set behind the center line.

Keep the feet in line with the target's center.

The arrow hits right of center.

The *tenouchi* is weak.

Bend the forefinger to take up the slack in the hand.

The front wrist is bent to the right.

Keep the wrist straight by aligning the bones of the wrist and arm. Do not rely on the wrist muscles to hold the bow in place.

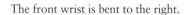

The front arm gives in at the release.

Stretch to the left and right from the center of the chest.

The right foot is set behind the center line.

Keep the feet in line with the target's center.

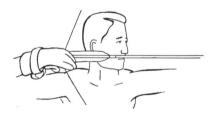

The arrow hits below center.

The arrow is held too high on the face.

Hold the arrow between the corner of the mouth and the bottom of the nose.

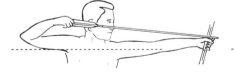

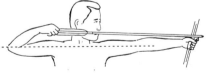

The right elbow is held too high in *kai*.

Keep both elbows parallel to the floor.

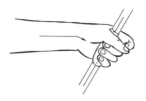

The left hand is bent downward.

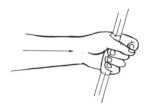

Keep the hand straight.

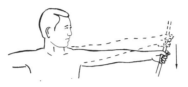

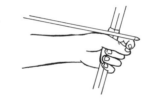

The front arm drops at the release.

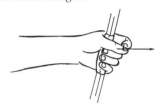

Push the left thumb toward the target's center.

Ashibumi is too narrow.

Widen the stance.

The grip is held too low.

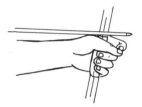

Hold the bow so that the arrow runs along the top edge of the grip.

The arrow hits above center.

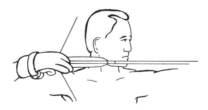

The arrow is held too low on the face.

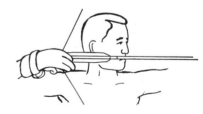

Hold the arrow between the corner of the mouth and the bottom of the nose.

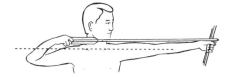 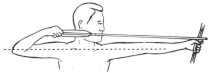

The right elbow is held too low in *kai*.

Keep both elbows parallel to the floor.

 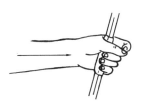

The left hand is bent upward.

Keep the hand straight.

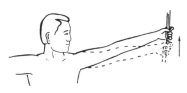 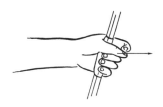

The front arm lifts at the release.

Push the left thumb toward the target's center.

Ashibumi is too wide.

Narrow the stance.

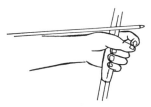 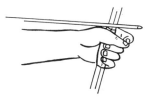

The grip is held too high.

Hold the bow so that the arrow runs along the top edge of the grip.

The arrows hit randomly.

Too much tension is placed in the hands when shooting.

Align the skeletal structure of the back, shoulders, and arms. Stretch evenly from the center of the body.

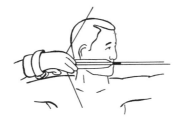 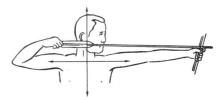

There is too much slack in the body.

Gently stretch the vertical and horizontal lines of the body.

  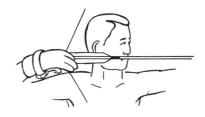

The arrow arcs smoothly but hits low.

The bow is not fully drawn.

Draw the bow until the *motohagi* is behind the corner of the mouth.

  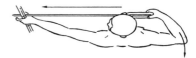

The arrow flight is erratic.

The arrow bends in *kai* because of excessive tension in the right hand.

Relax the right wrist. Draw the bow by setting the elbow behind the right shoulder.

The arrow is loosed by a forced opening of the right hand.

Do not rely on the muscles of the right hand to pull the bow. Stretch evenly from the center of the body until the release occurs naturally.

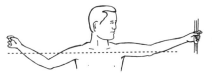  

The arms are uneven in *zanshin*.

There is excessive tension in the hands.

Relax the muscles. Align the skeletal structure of the back, shoulders, and arms. Stretch evenly from the center of the body.

 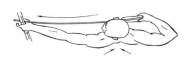 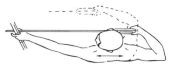

The body shakes uncontrollably in *kai*.

There is too much tension in the arms, shoulders, or chest.

In *daisan* remove all excessive tension from the body. Do not pull the bow with the arm muscles. Use the back muscles to simultaneously push and pull the bow.

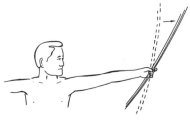 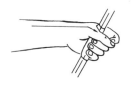 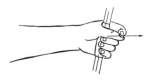

The bow casts forward at the release.

The left hand is bent downward because of excessive pressure against the "Y" of the thumb and forefinger.

Keep the wrist straight. Push the thumb toward the target's center.

 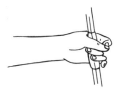 

The bow casts backward at the release.

The little finger is weak.

Make the last three fingers work as one. Gently squeeze the root of the thumb and the base of the little finger together.

The *yugaeri* does not occur.

The *tenouchi* is incorrect.

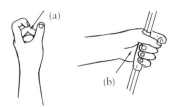

Leave a space between the bow and the last three fingers (a), and between the grip and the base of the thumb (b).

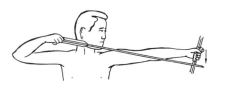

The arrow drops off the left hand in *hikiwake* or *kai.*

The right hand is not working properly.

Keep the right hand turned inward.

The face is turned into the arrow.

Keep the head straight.

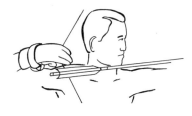

The arrow nock slips off the string.

The right wrist is bent or excessive tension is applied to the right hand.

Relax the right wrist and have the feeling that the string pulls the glove.

The *hazu* is cracked or the slot is not properly shaped.

Replace the *hazu*. Use a rattail file to make a keyhole-shaped slot.

At the release the string hits the inner arm.

The left hand is bent to the right.

Keep the hand straight.

The bow is held flat in the hand.

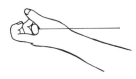

In *daisan* hold the bow at a slight angle. As you move into *kai* gradually increase the tension on the grip.

The left shoulder is thrust too far inward.

Keep both shoulders parallel to the arrow.

At the release the string hits the side of the face.

The head is turned to the right.

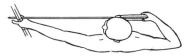

Keep the head straight.

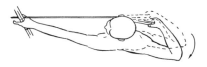

The bow is overdrawn.

Push and pull the bow evenly using the back muscles. Keep the right wrist straight and relaxed.

The left arm is held in place at the release.

At the release open from the center of the body so that the front arm moves a couple centimeters to the left.

 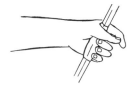 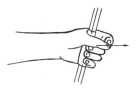

The bow drops in the hand at the release.

The bow is held too lightly.

Squeeze the grip with the lower fingers while pushing the thumb forward.

 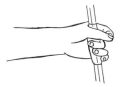 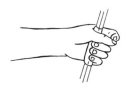

The bow drops out of the hand at the release.

The *tenouchi* is weak or the fingers are opened at the release in an attempt to make the *yugaeri* occur.

Keep the connection between the left thumb and the top of the middle finger.

 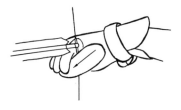 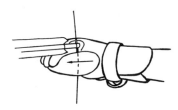

The string wear pattern on the glove is irregular or the glove leather is torn.

The thumb is held at an odd angle.

Set the string perpendicular to the thumb. Keep the right wrist straight when drawing the bow.

There is excessive tension in the right wrist.

Relax the wrist. Have the feeling that the string pulls the glove.

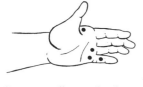

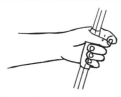

Blisters or callouses develop at selected points on the left hand.

The bow is held with excessive strength.

Hold the bow with just enough strength to keep it in place. An old teaching says, "Hold the bow like you would hold a baby's hand."

APPENDIX

Shiteimondo:
Student-Teacher Conversations

On February 20, 1990, before this book reached final publication, Onuma Hideharu sensei passed away. He was eighty years old. Onuma sensei was an exceptional man, with an exceptionally strong spirit. He was noble, dignified, and refined. A man of uncommon warmth and generosity, Onuma sensei was a true teacher in every sense of the word.

Sensei had two loves in life: kyudo and fishing. When he was not in the *kyudojo*, one would invariably find him at his favorite lake or pond. He once told me that he liked to go there to "not think." Sensei always said he was lucky at fishing. Not because he always caught fish, but because he almost never had to postpone a trip due to inclement weather. I can't count the times that I had warned him the night before a fishing trip of the probability of rain, then woke to find that the sun was up and so was he—happily anticipating his day at the lake. I used to ask myself this question: Did Sensei get up because the sun came out, or did the sun come out because he was up? The day he passed away I got my answer.

It was a dreary day, and raining lightly. Sensei had been semiconscious for some time, but that day he sat up in bed, asked for something to drink, then began very slowly to pull and release an imaginary bow. Then he settled back into his bed and closed his eyes. Sensei passed away a short time later.

Outside, the wind and rain intensified, blowing open the windows in the room. And later, as we prepared to take Sensei's body home, an earthquake shook the building. It was quite strong. So much so that we had to hold on to the bed to keep it from sliding across the room. It was late in the afternoon that together with Sensei's youngest daughter I accompanied the body home in the hearse. As we waited to leave, the rain worsened and the driver remarked that it would be a very difficult drive. Minutes later, the wind quieted and the rain slowed. We had no sooner left the hospital when the driver told us to look at the sky. There, arcing across the Tokyo skyline, was a magnificent double rainbow.

The drive home took about thirty minutes. On the way the rain stopped and the sky began to clear. By the time we reached home, the sun was setting and the sky had changed to a beautiful pink and blue color. My first thought was that Sensei must have gone fishing.

Onuma sensei taught me about kyudo. He taught me about spirit. He taught me how to live, and finally, he taught me how to die. His teaching is complete. Now I must spend the rest of my life trying to understand everything he taught me.

This final section, the *shiteimondo*, was assembled from the many hours of conversation that my wife, Jackie, and I had with Onuma sensei over the years that we lived and studied with him. We have included it in the belief that his words hold special value, and that others, like ourselves, will find his teaching and wisdom to be a constant source of inspiration.

Dan DeProspero

Dan: *Sensei, what should our highest purpose be in studying kyudo?*

Sensei: To perfect ourselves.

Dan: *Have you achieved perfection?*

Sensei: Of course not! It is not humanly possible to be perfect.

Dan: *If it is impossible, then why try?*

Sensei: Because to not try is to be less than human.

Dan: *Sensei, you often tell us that kyudo has the power to change us for the better. However, we have been practicing for some time now and I haven't noticed any real change in either Jackie or myself. How exactly does kyudo do this, and when can we expect to see some of the changes you talk about?*

Sensei: The answer is simple, but you will have to study it very carefully if it is to be of any value to you. Kyudo cannot really change us, we can only change ourselves. Kyudo is a metaphor for life. Shooting is merely a reflection of our true selves; how you are in life is how you will be in shooting. Someone who is sloppy and careless will have problems with the shooting procedure. One who is competitive and aggressive will compete with himself and others, and fight with the bow and arrow. People who have a tendency to focus their attention on one subject at the expense of all else will focus on hitting the target and ignore form and etiquette. Excuse-makers will make excuses. Boasters will boast. Kyudo itself cannot change all this, but it can make these things much more obvious to us. It then becomes our responsibility to recognize the problems and make the necessary changes.

Jackie: *Is this process similar to what you mean when you say that kyudo is the best way to subdue the ego?*

Sensei: Yes. Because shooting reveals the truth, and there is no way for me to hide my true ability from others. Eventually I must shoot. And when I do, anyone can see me as I truly am. In other arts, painting for example, even if I paint poorly I can say that my style is original. It is difficult, then, for others to judge. Of course, the art experts know the difference but most people do not have adequate training to judge if my painting is good or bad. In sports it is all too easy to blame a bad showing on your teammates or on an umpire's mistake. And even if you win, people can always say that your opponent was not in top condition. Those kinds of situations make it easy for us to avoid taking responsibility for our own shortcomings. But in kyudo there is only me, my equipment, and the target. I cannot blame my equipment because I alone am responsible for keeping it in good condition. I cannot blame the target because it is only paper and wood, and, though there are times when it seems to move to avoid the arrow, it does not do so. That means that I have no excuse, no escape from the truth, no one to blame but myself when the shooting does not go well. That knowledge is very humbling, and humility helps to keep our ego under control.

Dan: *Sensei, what makes a man a master?*

Sensei: I think a true master—one who is not so in title only—should have a generous heart. His nature should be such that he has a good effect on anyone he may come in contact with. My idea of a master is someone whose nature is such that he has the power to change his students' personalities. But I don't think many people are able to do this. As for myself, right now I just try to work on my own personality.

Dan: *Oh, Sensei, you're just being modest. After all, you just told us that humility is important.*

Sensei: Yes, humility is important, but so is honesty. I don't know, am I being honest or humble when I say this? I think honest. But if I say I'm honest then I'm not being humble, am I? [laughs]

Jackie: *Sensei, what is it about kyudo that has kept you so interested in it for so many years?*

Sensei: I have often wondered that myself. I think kyudo is so interesting because it is impossible to comprehend fully. Sometimes I feel like a blind turtle in the middle of the ocean searching for a log. Do you know what that means? It means to be in a hopeless situation. Sometimes kyudo makes you feel like that. It's funny how you can study for so long and still feel that you know so little. I know one thing, though, kyudo requires endless effort. Many times I have encountered obstacles in my training. But I found that if I persevered I always managed to break through. And once I am on the other side, things seem so clear and simple—I feel as if I can see farther and wider than before. I know that as long as I live there will always be obstacles to overcome. But I can never give up because on the other side lies a greater understanding of myself. And that makes all the effort worthwhile.

Jackie: *Sensei, I've heard you say that kyudo can add ten years to your life. But compared to sports or other martial arts there is very little physical exercise in the practice of kyudo.*

Sensei: Yes, that's true. But you are forgetting that health is something you must keep all your life and not just when you are young. Hard physical exercise is fine when you are twenty or thirty years old but there comes a time in your life when such kind of exercise is no longer healthy. Kyudo is something that you can practice your entire life. It helps improve your posture, circulation, and muscle tone. Also, you forget that mental health is equally important. Kyudo helps us develop and maintain an alert state of mind. In Japan, there are many people in their seventies or eighties who regularly practice kyudo. There is even a man of one hundred and one who still practices. I myself am close to eighty but I can still stand and sit straight, and stand up and sit down effortlessly. When I was young I was quite ill, so I am thoroughly convinced that my study of kyudo has allowed me to live at least ten years longer than would have been possible had I never practiced.

Jackie: *The other day you said that superstition has no place in kyudo. Could you explain what you meant by that?*

Sensei: You must make a distinction between superstition and faith. Having a belief in something is very important, but it must be positive. Many people have a favorite bow or set of arrows that they like to use—that's natural. But to come to depend on something to the point where you feel you are not your best without it is not good. It is negative, a sign of a weak spirit. This is what I mean by superstition. If your spirit is strong you need only rely on yourself and God to overcome any obstacle. This is what I mean by faith.

Dan: *You always say that the best way to learn how to shoot is to shoot. But what is the best way to develop a kyudo mind?*

Sensei: When your teacher shoots, watch him closely and shoot with him in your mind. If you do not have a teacher, make an image of a perfect teacher and shoot with that.

Dan: *Sensei, can you give us some advice on teaching?*

Sensei: Yes, don't overteach. These days many young instructors spend too much time explaining the fine points of shooting and ignore the overall appearance of the student. It is like trying to improve the cow by straightening its horns—you only end up killing the cow. It is better to work on the general health of the cow from the time it is young. Then, as it grows, the horns will straighten naturally.

Jackie: *In your opinion what is the single biggest problem people have in kyudo?*

Sensei: Oh, it is difficult to say since everyone is different. I think maybe the biggest problem is that most people shoot two-dimensionally. They tend to push and pull the bow along the line of the target. This makes the shooting flat. The bow must also move from front to back so that it surrounds the body. This adds another dimension to the shooting. But three-dimensional shooting really comes from the spirit. In kyudo the arms, feet, and body must be straight, but we must also have a round appearance. The roundness comes from the spirit being sent out in all directions. If people would remember this their kyudo would improve dramatically.

Dan: *I've noticed a great deal of difference between the way we practice kyudo and the way it is practiced in Japanese high schools and universities. Why is this?*

Sensei: School-level kyudo has a different purpose. It is mostly an outlet for the pressures of study. The students are taught the basics of shooting, but do not have so much emphasis put on the ceremonial or spiritual aspects of training. Later, if they wish to continue their practice of kyudo, they can study it more deeply.

Dan: *Sensei, how was practice different when you were young?*

Sensei: We didn't ask so many questions. [laughs]

Dan: *I'm sorry.*

Sensei: That's okay. I'm only joking. Questions are fine as long as you balance them with training. Actually, we didn't think about what kyudo was so much; we just did it. My father and then my father-in-law were both headmasters of Heki Ryu Sekka-ha, so from the time I was young I was surrounded by people doing kyudo. When I was little I played with the bow and arrows. My father never taught me about philosophy and the like. Mostly, I just watched him shoot and copied what I saw.

Jackie: *Sensei, you have told me in the past not to try to shoot like Dan. Do you mean that kyudo is different for men and women?*

Sensei: [laughing] I think maybe these days any answer I give will get me in trouble. What I mean is there are certain natural differences between men and women that must be respected. Women are blessed with a grace and beauty that is lacking in most men. Also, they are less prone to resort to the use of excessive strength. Therefore, women should take advantage of these qualities and not try to imitate men, who, for their part, must learn to be more graceful and use less strength. On the other hand, being too weak is also not good. I guess there is a point of balance between men and women that is neither too rigid nor too weak. That is what we all must search for.

Dan: *Sensei, at its highest level, what is kyudo to you?*

Sensei: At its very highest it is service rendered to God.

Dan: *I've heard you talk about God before. Do you think of God when you shoot?*

Sensei: I think that God has given me the talent and the opportunity to do kyudo. That was his gift to me. It is my responsibility, then, to study as hard as I can. And when I shoot I always try to make it as noble and elegant as I can because God is watching me. He expects me to do my best. And if I do so he will appreciate my effort and take over from there.

Dan: *Is that what you mean when you say "let God shoot for you?"*

Sensei: Yes, it is.

Dan: *Sensei, when you talk about God and kyudo it sounds like a religion.*

Sensei: No, kyudo is not a religion. But it does have many things in common with religion. It has ceremony and requires discipline. And we can use it to improve our personalities and develop a pure mind. These attributes have led some people to call it a "religion without words," but this only means that if your intentions are good and your heart is true, you should be able to influence, for the better, anyone who watches you shoot.

Dan: *You always talk of using kyudo to further peace and friendship. How do you reconcile this with the fact that the bow is a weapon?*

Sensei: First of all, our purpose is different from that of past archers. In Japan the bow has not been used as a weapon for centuries—not even for hunting. Instead, it was discovered that it was an excellent way for people to search for the truth inside themselves. This leads them to a better understanding not only of themselves but of others as well. And that is the first step to universal peace and friendship.

Dan: *You say that* hanare *is a thing of wonder, the greatest mystery in kyudo. Can you explain more about that?*

Sensei: It is just empty talk to discuss the mystery of *hanare*. It is impossible to understand. It has been compared to snow falling from a leaf or the moment when flint strikes iron, but even these explanations have no real meaning without firsthand experience of a true, natural *hanare*. Part of the problem is that *hanare* changes with age and experience. A young archer will have a powerful release [makes the sound "kan-paan"]. But an old master's release will be gentle [makes the sound "pe-tan"]. It is silly for young archers to imitate the release of the master—this only results in weak shooting. *Hanare* must come from inside you. As you are, so is your release. It cannot be taught. The only thing I can tell you is to try not to make the release, then one day the release will happen naturally on its own.

Jackie: *Why is kyudo such a good mental and spiritual discipline?*

Sensei: Kyudo is sometimes called "standing Zen." I think this means that, like Zen, it is very simple, but you must actively practice it to get anything of value from it. It is like writing the number "1" [a single horizontal stroke] in Japanese calligraphy; anyone can do it but to make a really vibrant and strong character takes a lifetime of practice. Kyudo is the same. Everything you are, or think you are, is reflected in your shooting. Therefore, you must have high ideals and pure thoughts. If you think about competing with others or try to impress those watching you, you will spoil your shooting. You must try to learn proper technique so that you can practice correctly. And after that you must spend your life trying to make your shooting pure. That, of course, is difficult because we are human and humans have so many faults. But...we try.

Dan: *Sensei, is it possible to overcome poor technique with a strong spirit?*

Sensei: Well, I think it is possible for the spirit to transcend technique. There are stories of people accomplishing great things through spirit alone. But I think we can only do this once. The second time around we would invariably fall back on our experiences, and that is how technique is born. For example, modern kyudo technique, which includes the *hassetsu* and ceremonial procedure, developed out of the experiences of great past masters. Ultimately, we must forget about technique, but forgetting about technique is not the same as never having learned it.

Jackie: *Sensei, why does the atmosphere of a* kyudojo *vary so much from place to place?*

Sensei: First of all, a *kyudojo* is like a home; it only reflects the character of the people who are in it. So some things, like kindness and courtesy, should be a part of every *kyudojo*. But to answer your question, the *yumi* has a long and varied history in Japan. It has been used for hunting and war, for court ceremony and games, for religious rituals, and for mental, physical, and spiritual development. With the exception of hunting and war, all of these are a part of kyudo today. Therefore, on a given day at a given *kyudojo*, the focus of training might be on any one of these areas. But balance is the key. Kyudo is a practice in balance, and a good *kyudojo* will reflect this. To focus entirely on one aspect or another is like viewing a wonderful painting through a tube. What you see may be nice but it is only a small part of the whole.

Dan: *Sensei, why do some people whose form is obviously poor consistently hit the target?*

Sensei: The answer is simple. Once they learn to place their arms and body in a position that allows them to hit the target, they never change. We call this *teppozuke* (rifle shooting), and it is the lowest form of shooting in kyudo. Such people are very accurate, but accuracy is all they have. Don't you think it is a little sad to spend your entire life practicing kyudo and have nothing more to show for it than the ability to shoot an arrow into a piece of paper? It is so much more rewarding to concentrate on correct form, technique, and attitude, and improve not only your accuracy but also your mental and physical self.

Jackie: *One of your old students once told us that there was a movement some years ago to get kyudo into the Olympics, and that you were among those who opposed the idea. Can you tell us why?*

Sensei: Oh, that was in 1964 when Japan hosted the Olympics. We Japanese were very anxious to do well in the Olympics that year and some thought that if we included kyudo as part of the archery competition we could surely win a gold medal. I opposed it for two reasons. First, when I was younger I studied Western archery and I knew that Western bows were technically superior to the Japanese *yumi.* Western bows are designed for accuracy. If you miss the mark it is possible to adjust the sight or different parts of the bow to improve your shooting. But kyudo is different. If we miss the mark in kyudo we must make adjustments in ourselves—our mind and body. I did not think it would have been a fair competition between the two styles. But more importantly, I was afraid that if kyudo became a regular part of the Olympics it would lose its traditional focus— the triumph of mind over matter.

Jackie: *In Western archery we can determine the best archers by looking at their scores. What is the best way to judge a good archer in kyudo?*

Sensei: Kyudo makes a distinction between skillful shooting and correct shooting. Skillful shooting is always accurate, but so is correct shooting. Instead of watching the target you should watch the archer. Is his body straight? Is he relaxed? Are his movements clean and efficient? Does he blink or move unnecessarily? At the release, does he make you feel like his arrow has pierced your soul? These are the things you should look for in a kyudo archer.

Jackie: *What do you look for in a complete beginner?*

Sensei: Mostly I look for students who are sincere and courteous. That comes first. They also should have a neat, clean appearance. If they cannot take the time and effort to keep themselves tidy then they certainly will not have the patience to learn kyudo. Good students listen carefully to everything they are told. They are humble when praised, and make no excuses when corrected. The very best students need only be told something once. They are like a blank sheet of paper— open and ready to accept the information that is presented to them.

Dan: *Sensei, you have told us on more than one occasion that we must find the secrets that lie hidden within kyudo, but you rarely tell us what to look for. How will we know these secrets when we find them?*

Sensei: They are obvious, just simple truths. Trust me, you will know them when you find them. But you must be the one to search for them. All I can do is point you in the right direction. Even if I tell you everything I have found it is no use to you unless you discover it yourself. What value are diamonds to you if you have only heard the story of their being found? Remember a few years ago when I told you how the target appears to come closer and closer until it touches the end of the arrow? For the longest time you tried to imagine it happening, but because it was only a story it held no real value for you. Then one day you experienced it in the way that I meant and you immediately knew the difference between experiencing the truth and imagining it. It may be a long time before you have the experience again, but when you do the truth of it will be obvious.

Dan: *Sensei, you have been practicing kyudo for over seventy years now, but I've heard you say many times that you are still a beginner. With all your experience, how can you say that you are a beginner?*

Sensei: It is all a matter of perspective. In a way it is like climbing a mountain. It is the same mountain for both of us but I started climbing before you. You look ahead and see me where you would like to be. If I allow myself to look back then I can see that in comparison with you I have come a long way. But I don't like to look back because it stops my own progress. Just like you, I always look forward. And because of that I, too, feel like a beginner. But this is not a bad thing because being a beginner means that fresh and exciting challenges lie ahead.

Jackie: *I have heard people say that testing is not important in kyudo, but you have always encouraged us to try for tests. Why is this?*

Sensei: [smiles] Many people misunderstand the purpose of a test. They think only of passing the test to improve their grade. That is meaningless. I encourage you to take the kyudo gradings because it is important for you to periodically test your mental, physical, and technical abilities. It is all too easy to become comfortable with one's shooting in daily practice. Sometimes we need the added pressure of a test or demonstration or some other special event to reveal the truth about ourselves. Tests are especially useful because you learn a little when you pass, but you learn a great deal more when you fail.

Jackie: *What do the examiners look for in a test?*

Sensei: It depends. At the lower levels they look for a clear understanding of the basics. At the higher levels the strength of one's character takes on more importance. Also, as a person progresses, his or her form and movement should appear more natural. Too much *kamae* (posturing) is considered crude. It is like a *fugu* (blowfish): On the outside it is sharp and powerful looking, but inside it is only air.

Dan: *Can you tell us what the masters look for in each other's shooting?*

Sensei: In the person they look for depth of character and dignity. In the shooting they look for refined technique and *hibiki*, a kind of aftershock of *ki* that hits all who are present.

Jackie: *We have been extremely lucky to have had the opportunity to live and study with you for all these years. Someday, though, we will have to return home. How can we practice so that we will be able to continue along the right path without your constant advice and supervision?*

Sensei: As far as shooting is concerned it is necessary to periodically return to the basics. But perhaps more importantly, your practice should always center around these six elements: truth, goodness, beauty, balance, humility, and perseverance.

Dan: *Sensei, what is the most important thing that kyudo has given you?*

Sensei: I think kyudo has given me a great deal. I'm very lucky. But the thing I value most is the friendship of all the people I have met through kyudo. As I grow older I am losing my strength, and my body is robbing me of my ability to do kyudo in the way that I would like. That makes me a little sad, but it is nice to know that as long as I live I will always have my friends.

BIBLIOGRAPHY

Acker, William R.B. *Japanese Archery*. Rutland/Tokyo: Charles E. Tuttle Co., 1965.

Aikens, C. Melvin, and Higuchi, Takayasu. *Prehistory of Japan*. New York: Harcourt, Brace, Jovanovich Publications, 1985.

Anzawa, Toko (Heijiro). *Dai Sha Do*. Tokyo: Shatokutei, 1970.

Draeger, Donn F. *Classical Budo*. New York/Tokyo: Weatherhill, 1973.

Hall, John Whitney. *Japan from Prehistory to Modern Times*. Tokyo: Charles E. Tuttle Co., 1984.

Herrigel, Eugen. *Zen in the Art of Archery*. Translated by R.F.C. Hull. New York: Random House, Inc., 1971.

Inagaki, Genshiro. *Kyudo Nyumon*. Tokyo: Tokyo Shoten, 1978.

Ishikawa, Takashi. *Kokoro: The Soul of Japan*. Tokyo: The East Publications, Inc., 1986.

Ishioka, Hisao, and Kawamura, Yuriyuki. *Kyudo Nyumon*. Tokyo: Aikodo, 1977.

Leggett, Trevor. *Zen and the Ways*. Boulder, Colorado: Shambala Publications, Inc., 1978.

Ochiai, Seikichi, and Onuma, Hideharu. *Japanese Archery*. Tokyo: Asahi Archery Co. Ltd., 1961.

Ogasawara, Kiyonobu. *Kyudo*. Tokyo: Kodansha, 1974.

Random, Michel. *The Martial Arts*. London: Octopus Books, 1978.

Sato, Kaori. "Nichi Getsu Shin." Manuscript. Lyon/Tokyo, 1990.

Sunohara, Heihachiro. *Gendai Kyudo Shojiten*. Tokyo: Asahi Shobo, 1966.

Suzuki, Daisetz T. *Zen and Japanese Culture*. Bollingen series LXIV. New York: Princeton University Press, 1973.

Uno, Yozaburo, ed. *Gendai Kyudo Koza*. 7 vols. Tokyo: Yuzankaku Shupan K.K., 1982.

Uragami, Hiroko. *Shoshinsha no Tame no Kyudo*. Tokyo: Seibido Shupan, 1974.

Yurino, Minoru, ed. *Kyudo Hassetsu: Eight Points in Japanese Archery*. Tokyo: Zen Nippon Kyudo Renmei, 1981.

Zen Nihon Kyudo Renmei. *Kyudo Kyohon*. 4 vols. Tokyo: Zen Nihon Kyudo Renmei, 1984.

DIRECTORY

AUSTRALIA

Meishin Dojo
Neil Ringe
P.O. Box 412
Byron Bay 2481
N.S.W.
Tel: (066) 858-673

Park, David
27 Holloway Road
Brunswick 3056
Victoria
Tel: (03) 387-7815

Pearse, Jeremy
24 Dalton Avenue
Aldcate 5154
South Australia

AUSTRIA

Hammerschick, Peter
Eignerstrasse 2
A-4020 Linz
Tel: 0732 537044
Fax: 0732 782652

Oesterreich Kyudo
Verein Schwenderg 3/12
1150 Vienna
TEl: 0222-8348502

FINLAND

Finnish Kyudo Federation
Kari Laine, President
Piispantie 8A 14
00370 Helsinki
Tel/Fax: 358 (9) 0 551190

Espoo

Tapiolan Karate Dojo/Kyudo
Kaj Westersund
Sepontie 3 J 59
02130 Espoo
Tel: 358 (9) 0 465236

Helsinki

Hikari
Virva Ohtonen, President
Pengerkatu 20 B 31
00500 Helsinki
Tel: 358 (9) 0 60906480

Lapua

Lapuan
Virkiä/Budosection/Kyudo
Risto Jalava
Tikantie 5
62100 Lapua
Tel: 358 (9) 64 4387485

Porvoo

Yosaiki
Leif Bagge, President
Jousitie 10 D 27
06150 Porvoo
Tel: 358 (9) 15 668531

Tampere

Haya
Jussi Pakkanen
Kiertotie 25
36200 Kangasala

FRANCE

Centre de Kyudo du Taillé
La Riaille
Jyoji Frey
F-07800 St Laurent du Pape
Tel: (33) 75 85 10 39
Fax: (33) 75 85 39 49

Dojo Asahi
Michel Martin
25 rue Pétion
75011 Paris
Tel: 43 56 07 19

Lyon Meishin Dojo- Shiseikan
Michel Chavret
22 rue des Jardins

69100 Villeurbanne
Tel: (33) 78 80 24 68

Meitoku Dojo
Languedocian Kyudo
Association
Marie-Thérèse Kolmer
Le Mail des Abbés
304 rue Max Mousseron
34000 Montpellier
Tel: 67 72 44 30

Paris Shatoku-Tei
6 rue du Port aux Dames
91200 Draveil

GERMANY

DJB-Sektion Kyudo
Feliks F. Hoff
Volksdorfer Weg 50 R
2 Hamburg 65
Tel/Fax: 040-6405795

Baden

Elsen, Stefan
Dürrbachstr. 24
75 Karlsruhe 41
Tel: 0721-408066

Bayern

Böhm, Kurt
Liegnitzerstr. 55
895 Kaufbeuren
Tel: 08341-5145

Isar Dojo e.V. München
Lilo Reinhardt, President
Deidesheimer Str. 22
W-8000 München 40
Tel: 089-3002547

Berlin

Baer, Thomas
Donnersmarckallee 37
1 Berlin 28
Tel: 030-4017866

Bremen

Müller, Günter
Kämenadenweg 9a
28 Bremen 41
Tel: 0421-426935

Hamburg

Zimmermann, Sven
Hirschgraben 38
2 Hamburg 76
Tel: 040-2500190

Hessen

Ibel, Johannes
Linnèstr. 19
6 Frankfurt 60
Tel: 069-436630

Niedersachsen

Hasselmann, Hans
Teichstr. 36
32 Hildesheim
Tel: 05121-134167

Bever, Manfred
Breite Str. 2
4775 Lippetal/Oestinghausen
Tel: 02923-8254

Nordrhein-Westfalen

Steinmetz, Gerald
Lousbergstr. 42 B
51 Aachen
Tel: 0241-155652

Rhein-Hessen

Lindemeyer, Rolf
Adam Karrillonstr. 49-51
65 Mainz
Tel: 06131-670901

Rheinland-Pfalz

Eicher, Fritz
Altenbacherstr. 24
6702 Bad Dürkheim 5
Tel: 06322-65931

Saarland

Linneberger, Jürgen
Am Weiher 2
6625 Püttlingen 3
Tel: 06806-45049

Schleswig-Holstein

Steinhauer, Uwe
An der Hülshorst 4

24 Lübeck
Tel: 0451-34462

Württemburg

Beutnagel, Uwe
Spreuergasse 11
7 Stuttgart 50
Tel: 0711-564554

ICELAND

Sigurdsson, Tryggvi
Laugateigur 35
105 Reykjavik
Tel: 354-1-33431
Fax: 354-1-641753

ITALY

Artegna (Udine)

Forconi, Dino
Via Udine 21
Artegna (Udine)

Milan

Ai Kyudo
Ruggero Paracchini, President
Kyudo Club Torino, Instructor
Via Civitali 69
20148 Milano
Tel: 02-406575

Kenzan Dojo (Gallarate)
Rosenberg Colorni, Vittorio
Via Giuseppe Frua 12
20146 Milano
Tel: 02-468778
Tel: 0321-957410 (Ren
Shin Kan Kyudojo)

Kyudo Club il
Gabbiano (Padova)
Antonio Rocchi
Via Cuore Immacolato
di Maria 4
20141 Milano
Tel: 02-8433671

Kyudo Club Insai (Milano)
Yoshihiro Ichikura
52 Alzaia Naviglio Pavese
20100 Milano
Tel: 02-8377736

Kyudo Club Vittuone (Milano)
Sergio Masocco
Via A. Grandi 16

20018 Vittuone (Milano)
Tel: 02-9023168

Mozzate (Como)

Kenzan Dojo (Gallarate)
Mario Foglia
Via Parini 5
22076 Mozzate (Como)
Tel: 0331-830538

Rome

Accademia Romana Kyudo
Placido Processi, President
Via Castelnuovo 44
00165 Roma
Tel: 06-6374834

Aka Tondo (Roma)
Francesco Ravizza
Via Alessandro Torlonia 41
00161 Roma
Tel: 06-8411393

Heki Danjou
Masatsugu (Roma)
Luigi Genzini
Viale Gorgia di Lentini 330
00124 Casalpalocco (Roma)
Tel: 06-6093431

JAPAN

Asahi Archery Co., Ltd.
Ohtsuka Archery Mansion
Minami Ohtsuka 3-23-3
Toshima ku, Tokyo 170
Tel: (03) 3986-2301
Fax: (03) 3986-2302

DeProspero, Dan and Jackie
Ohtsuka Archery
Mansion #406
Minami Ohtsuka 3-23-3
Toshima-ku, Tokyo 170
Tel/Fax: (03) 3986-9751
also see United States listing

Zen Nihon Kyudo Renmei
Kishi Kinen Taiikukan Bldg.
1-1-1 Jinnan
Shibuya-ku, Tokyo
Tel: (03) 3481-2387
Fax: (03) 3481-2398

NETHERLANDS

Kyudo Renmei Nederland
Postbus 15189
3501 BD Utrecht

Buurman, Kees
Nieuwe Rijn 89
2312 JL Leiden
Tel: 071-140088

Lap, Wouter
Heiligeweg 106
1561 DL Krommenie
Tel: 075-216679

Möricke, Harald
Knibbeldijk 4
7245 NG Laren Gld.
Tel: 05738-1550

Saat, Malou
Molenwerfsteeg 3
3514 BZ Utrecht
Tel: 030-713040

Stelwagen, Henk
Wobbemalaene 6
8816 HZ Schingen Frl.
Tel: 05172-2183

Wekker, Hans de
Dorpsstraat 4
9474 TA Zuidlaarderveen
Tel/Fax: 05989-1816

SPAIN

International Contacts

Asociacion Espanola de Kyudo
Conrad J. Daubanton
President
Enrique Gimenez 1, 1-B
08034 Barcelona
Tel: 34 (3) 204 33 47

Spanish Contacts

Asociacion Espanola de Kyudo
Juan Carlos Acin, Secretary
Don Pedro de Luna 44
Principal
50010 Zaragoza
Tel: 34 (76) 33 02 90

SWITZERLAND

Association Helvetique de Kyudo
Charles Stampfli, President
73 B Ch. des Verjus

Ch-1212 Grand Lancy/Geneve
Tel: 022/794 17 68
Fax: 022/794 76 00

Basel

Bader, Joerg
Unterer Rebbergweg 18
4151 Reinach/Basel
Tel: 061/711 45 68

Jud, Markus
Rosentalstrasse 71
4058 Basel
Tel: 061/692 62 28

Bern

Müller-Miura, Christoph
Steckweg 9
CH-3014 BERN
Tel/Fax: 031/372 33 32

Schneider, Martin
Stathalterstrasse 33
3018 Bern
Tel: 031/55 19 49

Serquet, Jean-Marc
50 Chemin Vert
2502 Bienne/Bern
Tel: 032/41 40 17

Geneva

Horta, Emmanuel
111 rue de Geneve
1226 Thonex/Geneve
Tel: 022/349 62 68

Perez, Ma-I
1 Samuel Constant
1209 Geneve
Tel: 022/345 37 75

Lucern

Schmidiger, Kurt
Dattenmattstrasse 23
6010 Kriens
Tel: 041/41 59 22

Vaud

Berrocosa, Jose
La "Chaussia" 2C
1616 Attalens/Vaud
Tel: 021/947 54 10

Reymond, Philippe
9 Ch. de la Fontanettaz
1009 Pully/Vaud
Tel: 021/28 84 86

Zurich

Anke, Dieter
Frohburgweg 3
8180 Buelach/Zurich
Tel: 01/860 83 75
Fax: 01/438 71 20

UNITED KINGDOM

British Association for
Japanese Archery
(Dai Ei Kyudo Renmei)
John Bush
95 Court Road
London SE9 5AG
Tel: 081-859-1303
Fax: 081-317-7188

Cardiff Dojo, Wales
John Davies
17 Little Mill
Whitechurch, Cardiff
South Wales
Tel: 0222 617184

Chalfont St. Giles Dojo
Doug Jones
Buckinghamshire
(North London)
Tel: 0923 770913

Liphook Dojo
Peter Humm
5 Mill Lane, Passfield
Liphook, Hampshire
GV30 7RP
Tel: 0428 571472

London Kyudo Group
Liam O'Brien
2 Longfield Road, Ealing
London W5 2DH
Tel: 081-998-9438

Macmillan, Timothy
18 Westmoreland Street
Bath BA2 3HE
Tel: 225-334981

Meishin Kyudo Kai
Mascalls School Sports Hall
Gedges Hill
Paddock Wood, Kent

White Rose Foundation Dojo
Darenth
Don Slade-Southham
Park, Kent (South London)
Tel: 032-222-2145
Fax: 081-317-7188

UNITED STATES

Arizona

Tucson Kyudo Kai
Bill Savary
2234 N. Ralph
Tucson, AZ 85712
Tel: (602) 323-2954

California

Northern California
Kyudo Federation
Earl Hartman, President
250 Ventura
Palo Alto, CA 94306
Tel: (415) 494-1584

Florida

DeProspero, Dan and Jackie
25 Lake Henry Drive
Lake Placid, FL 33852
Tel: (813) 465-4906
also see Japan listing

Georgia

Georgia Kyudo Renmei
Edwin C. Symmes, Jr
President
P.O. Box 8101
Atlanta, GA 30306
Tel: (404) 876-7260

Hawaii

Hawaii Kyudo Kai
Bishop Gyokuei Matsuura,
President
1708 Nuuanu Avenue
Honolulu, HI 96817
Tel: (808) 533-2518

Indiana

Indiana Kyudo Renmei
COL Philip Swain, President
Route 1, Box 177D
Lizton, IN 46149
Tel: (317) 994-5180

INDEX